Amel Selmi

Grundwissen Englisch inklusiv

Wortschatz 6. Klasse Inklusionsmaterial

Die Autorin

Amel Selmi ist seit Jahren im Gemeinsamen Lernen aktiv. Seit 2011 unterrichtet sie Kinder mit und ohne sonderpädagogischen Unterstützungsbedarf in den Fächern Englisch und Sport. Ihre verfassten Titel basieren auf langjährigen Erfahrungen, die sie an unterschiedlichen Schulen und Schulformen sammeln konnte, und ermöglichen die praktische Umsetzung inklusiven Unterrichts – aus der Praxis für die Praxis. Im Rahmen der konzeptionellen Ausrichtung erstellt Amel Selmi Vorschläge und Konzepte, wie Inklusion effektiv und schülerorientiert umgesetzt werden kann.

1. Auflage 2022
© 2022 PERSEN Verlag, Hamburg

AAP Lehrerwelt GmbH
Veritaskai 3
21079 Hamburg
Telefon: +49 (0) 40325083-040
E-Mail: info@lehrerwelt.de
Geschäftsführung: Christian Glaser
USt-ID: DE 173 77 61 42
Register: AG Hamburg HRB/126335
Alle Rechte vorbehalten.

Das Werk als Ganzes sowie in seinen Teilen unterliegt dem deutschen Urheberrecht. Der Erwerber einer Einzellizenz des Werkes ist berechtigt, das Werk als Ganzes oder in seinen Teilen für den eigenen Gebrauch und den Einsatz im eigenen Präsenz- wie auch dem Distanzunterricht zu nutzen.
Produkte, die aufgrund ihres Bestimmungszweckes zur Vervielfältigung und Weitergabe zu Unterrichtszwecken gedacht sind (insbesondere Kopiervorlagen und Arbeitsblätter), dürfen zu Unterrichtszwecken vervielfältigt und weitergegeben werden.

Die Nutzung ist nur für den genannten Zweck gestattet, nicht jedoch für einen schulweiten Einsatz und Gebrauch, für die Weiterleitung an Dritte einschließlich weiterer Lehrkräfte, für die Veröffentlichung im Internet oder in (Schul-)Intranets oder einen weiteren kommerziellen Gebrauch.
Mit dem Kauf einer Schullizenz ist die Schule berechtigt, die Inhalte durch alle Lehrkräfte des Kollegiums der erwerbenden Schule sowie durch die Schülerinnen und Schüler der Schule und deren Eltern zu nutzen.

Nicht erlaubt ist die Weiterleitung der Inhalte an Lehrkräfte, Schülerinnen und Schüler, Eltern, andere Personen, soziale Netzwerke, Downloaddienste oder Ähnliches außerhalb der eigenen Schule.
Eine über den genannten Zweck hinausgehende Nutzung bedarf in jedem Fall der vorherigen schriftlichen Zustimmung des Verlags.
Sind Internetadressen in diesem Werk angegeben, wurden diese vom Verlag sorgfältig geprüft. Da wir auf die externen Seiten weder inhaltliche noch gestalterische Einflussmöglichkeiten haben, können wir nicht garantieren, dass die Inhalte zu einem späteren Zeitpunkt noch dieselben sind wie zum Zeitpunkt der Drucklegung. Der PERSEN Verlag übernimmt deshalb keine Gewähr für die Aktualität und den Inhalt dieser Internetseiten oder solcher, die mit ihnen verlinkt sind, und schließt jegliche Haftung aus.

Wir verwenden in unseren Werken eine genderneutrale Sprache. Wenn keine neutrale Formulierung möglich ist, nennen wir die weibliche und die männliche Form. In Fällen, in denen wir aufgrund einer besseren Lesbarkeit nur ein Geschlecht nennen können, achten wir darauf, den unterschiedlichen Geschlechtsidentitäten gleichermaßen gerecht zu werden.

Autorin:	Amel Selmi
Covergrafik:	Stefan Lucas
Illustrationen:	Julia Flasche, Katharina Reichert-Scarborough, Corina Beurenmeister, Steffen Jähde, Barbara Gerth, Wibke Brandes, Bettina Weyland, Tania Schnagl/Robert Plötz, Mele Brink, Antje Bohnstedt, Sandra Schmidt, Anke Fröhlich, Carla Miller, Christina Piper, Ingrid Hecht, Petra Lefin, Manuela Ostadal, Daniela Bühnen, Elisabeth Lottermoser, Stefan Lohr, Anja Ley, Rebecca Meyer, Wolfgang Slawski, Kristina Klotz, Stefan Lucas, Satzpunkt Ursula Ewert GmbH
Satz:	Satzpunkt Ursula Ewert GmbH, Bayreuth
Druck und Bindung:	Design and printing JSC KOPA, Litauen

ISBN: 978-3-403-20774-0
www.persen.de

Inhaltsverzeichnis

Vorwort / Methodisch-didaktische Hinweise .. 5

1 food

word bank	7
food at the market and in the restaurant 1	10
food at the market and in the restaurant 2	11
food at the market and in the restaurant 3	12
food at the market and in the restaurant 1	13
food at the market and in the restaurant 2	14
food at the market and in the restaurant 3	15
healthy and unhealthy food 1	16
healthy and unhealthy food 2	17
healthy and unhealthy food 3	18
healthy and unhealthy food 1	19
healthy and unhealthy food 2	20
healthy and unhealthy food 3	21
guessing game	22
guessing game	24

2 school holidays

word bank	26
countries and activities 1	29
countries and activities 2	30
countries and activities 3	31
countries and activities 4	32
countries and activities 5	33
countries and activities 6	34
countries and activities 1	35
countries and activities 2	36
countries and activities 3	37
countries and activities 4	38
countries and activities 5	39
countries and activities 6	40

3 my school day

word bank	41
my school day 1	44
my school day 2	45
my school day 3	46
my school day 4	47
my school day 5	48
my school day 6	49
my school day 7	50
my school day 1	51
my school day 2	52
my school day 3	53
my school day 4	54
my school day 5	55
my school day 6	56
my school day 7	57

4 animals and pets

word bank	58
animals and pets 1	61
animals and pets 2	62
animals and pets 3	63
animals and pets 4	64
animals and pets 1	65
animals and pets 2	66
animals and pets 3	67
animals and pets 4	68
at the zoo 1	69
at the zoo 2	70
at the zoo 1	71
at the zoo 2	72

5 prepositions

word bank	73
prepositions 1	78
prepositions 2	79
prepositions 3	80
prepositions 4	81
prepositions 5	82
prepositions 6	83
prepositions 7	84
prepositions 1	85
prepositions 2	86
prepositions 3	87
prepositions 4	88
prepositions 5	89
prepositions 6	90
prepositions 7	91

Inhaltsverzeichnis

6 numbers

word bank	92
numbers 1	94
numbers 2	95
numbers 1	96
numbers 2	97

7 the date

word bank	98
the date 1	100
the date 2	101
the date 1	102
the date 2	103

8 English in action

word bank	104
classroom phrases 1	108
classroom phrases 2	109
classroom phrases 1	110
classroom phrases 2	111
classroom phrases 3	112

Grau unterlegte Arbeitsblätter im Inhaltsverzeichnis sind die Arbeitsblätter für die Lernenden mit sonderpädagogischem Förderbedarf.

Digitales Zusatzmaterial: Lösungen als PDF-Datei

Vorwort / Methodisch-didaktische Hinweise

Das vorliegende Übungsbuch eignet sich für die 6. Jahrgangsstufe und ist für inklusiven Englischunterricht ausgelegt. Es beinhaltet alle vorgesehenen Themen und Anforderungen des Lehrplans für die Klasse 6 und deckt somit den gesamten hier zu erlernenden Wortschatzbereich ab. Themenbezogen angelehnt an das Lehrwerk ermöglicht es den Schülerinnen und Schülern, mithilfe unterschiedlicher Übungen Vokabeln zu erlernen sowie den erlernten Wortschatz zu vertiefen und zu wiederholen.

Eine individuelle Unterrichtsgestaltung steht hierbei im Mittelpunkt, sodass die Materialien in unterschiedlich strukturierten Klassen eingesetzt und spezifisch auf die jeweiligen Lerngruppen abgestimmt werden können. Insbesondere inklusive Klassen mit heterogenen Lerngeschwindigkeiten und Förderniveaus profitieren vom Einsatz der hier vorliegenden Kopiervorlagen. Leistungsübergreifende Kooperation und gemeinsames Lernen wird auch innerhalb der Differenzierung gefördert. Eine übersichtliche Darstellung des Vokabulars ermöglicht den Schülerinnen und Schülern, die jeweilige Unterrichtsthematik der Fachbücher schnell zu erfassen und zu vertiefen. Lehrerinnen und Lehrern werden Materialien an die Hand gegeben, um auf eine einfache Art strukturiert, binnendifferenziert und individualisiert jahrgangsspezifische Themen zu üben und zu vertiefen.

Methodisch-didaktische Hinweise

1. Sprache und Kommunikation

Für Fremdsprachen und somit auch für den Englischunterricht ist das Erlernen eines Wortschatzes unabdingbar, um elementare Kommunikationsstrategien auszuführen, Texte zu verstehen und überhaupt in Kommunikation treten zu können. Durch die in diesem Übungsband in thematische Zusammenhänge geordneten Vokabeln erlernen Schülerinnen und Schüler früh, ihren Grundwortschatz zu erweitern und sich in alltagsbezogenen Themen zu verständigen und mitzuteilen. Diese Struktur und die Kombination mit bildlichen Darstellungen ermöglichen ein vereinfachtes Aneignen und spontanes Nachschlagen von Vokabeln, dessen Einsatz die Grundlage dafür bildet, eine Fremdsprache anwenden und somit kommunizieren zu können.

2. Kompetenzerwartungen

Dieser Band ist in Anlehnung an die Kompetenzerwartungen der 6. Jahrgangsstufe ausgerichtet. Kleinschrittig werden der Lernstoff, die vorgesehenen Themen, Inhalte und entsprechenden Arbeitsaufträge abgedeckt.

Die Schülerinnen und Schüler können …

- sich zum Thema *food* äußern
- *school holidays* und *activities* beschreiben
- Schule und Stundenplan gestalten
- über ihre Hobbys und ihre Freizeitgestaltung berichten
- Tiere (*pets, animals, wild animals*) unterscheiden und benennen
- Zahlen und Ordnungszahlen sowie das Datum schreiben
- zu relevanten Themen einen kreativen Text schreiben
- Präpositionen richtig anwenden
- *classroom phrases* äußern.

3. Inklusion und Lernen

Die in diesem Band vorliegenden Übungen und Texte sind mit besonderer Berücksichtigung der Bedürfnisse eines inklusiven Unterrichts erstellt worden. Diese Unterrichtsform stellt viele Lehrerinnen und Lehrer vor große Herausforderungen, da alle Schülerinnen und Schüler möglichst individuell und leistungsdifferent gefördert werden sollen. Doch ist dies besonders im fremdsprachlichen Bereich mit bisherigen Lehrwerken schwierig umzusetzen, wenn nicht sogar fast unmöglich. Aus diesem Grund ist dieses Vokabel-Übungsbuch derart gestaltet worden, inklusiven Unterricht für Lehrkräfte und auch für die Lernenden leistungsheterogen und in seiner Struktur vereinheitlicht nachhaltig zu ermöglichen.

Aufgrund der unterschiedlichen Aufgabentypen und Niveau-Differenzierungen können die Kopiervorlagen für den gesamten Klas-

Methodisch-didaktische Hinweise

senverband kopiert werden. Die übersichtliche Strukturierung der Inhalte und Themen bietet den Lehrerinnen und Lehrern einen schnellen Zugriff auf Materialien sowohl für lernstarke als auch lernschwache Schülerinnen und Schüler. So eignet sich dieser Band hervorragend zum Einsatz in inklusiven Lerngruppen. Aber auch unabhängig davon können diese Materialien für Klassen unterschiedlicher Lernniveaus eingesetzt werden. Die sich unterscheidenden Übungen helfen, mehr Sicherheit in den verschiedenen Leistungsniveaus im Umgang mit dem englischen Wortschatz zu erlangen, das Vokabular zu erweitern und zu vertiefen. Hierbei motivieren klar strukturierte Lerneinheiten zum Arbeiten und bieten besonders für lernschwache Schülerinnen und Schüler einen vereinfachten Zugang, um Lerninhalte zu erfassen und die Übungen umzusetzen. Dies wurde so umgesetzt, dass die Kopiervorlagen für Schülerinnen und Schüler mit Förderbedarf weniger abstrakt und durch Vereinfachungen oder Unterstützung angeleitet sind. Viele Illustrationen, Vorgaben, Beispielsätze und Einsatzübungen unterstützen den Prozess, den Unterrichtsstoff inklusiv und zeitgleich zu vermitteln. Kapitel für Kapitel werden das wichtige Vokabular wiederholt und vielfältige Übungen zur Vertiefung des Wortschatzes angeboten. Ebenfalls werden die Schreibkompetenzen durch das Schreiben von freien Texten gefördert. Die *word banks* zu Beginn der Kapitel bieten die Möglichkeit, das Vokabular schnell zu überschauen und zu lernen.

4. Zu den Übungen

Im vorliegenden Übungsbuch werden unterschiedliche Übungen und Texte angeboten: Einsetzübungen, Zuordnungsübungen, Bildbeschreibungen und kurze Texte mit Fragen zum Verständnis.

Die Übungen sind unabhängig vom Lehrwerk einsetzbar, decken jedoch die spezifischen und lehrwerkrelevanten Themen ab. Sie sind sowohl für lernstarke als auch für lernschwache Gruppen konzipiert. Es ist zudem jederzeit möglich, lernschwache Gruppen auch die schwierigeren Kopiervorlagen bearbeiten zu lassen, wenn der Lernstoff beherrscht wird und der Wortschatz vertieft werden soll. Kopiervorlagen für lernschwache Schülerinnen und Schüler sind zum besseren Verständnis zusätzlich mit zweisprachigen Aufgabenanleitungen versehen. Bitte beachten Sie, dass die Erläuterung der Aufgaben zum besseren Verständnis und zur besseren Lesbarkeit sinngemäß und nicht wortwörtlich übersetzt wurde. Das erleichtert den lernschwächeren Schülerinnen und Schülern die Arbeit erheblich und versetzt sie in die Lage, die Aufgaben selbstständig zu bearbeiten.

5. Merkmale auf einen Blick

- Abdeckung aller schulrelevanten Themen der 6. Jahrgangsstufe
- einfache und klare Strukturierung
- ermöglicht selbstständiges Arbeiten
- Vokabelliste (*word bank*) zu jedem Thema
- themenbezogenes Vokabular
- eignet sich zur systematischen Wiederholung und Festigung des Wortschatzes
- Übungsmaterial sowohl für regulären als auch für Unterricht in Inklusionsklassen (für Lernende mit Förderbedarf geeignet)
- kleinschrittige und vereinfachte Aufgaben
- leistungsdifferenziertes Arbeitsmaterial
- zweisprachige Arbeitsaufträge für leistungsschwächere Schülerinnen und Schüler
- unterstützende Illustrationen

Bedeutung der Aufgabennummerierung

① Aufgaben mit dieser Markierung sind für Regelschüler und -schülerinnen konzipiert worden, das heißt für Lernende, die nach den Anforderungen der allgemeinen Schule unterrichtet und bewertet werden. Sie orientieren sich an den allgemeingültigen Kompetenzen für den Englischunterricht.

❷ Aufgaben mit dieser Markierung sind für Förderschüler und -schülerinnen entwickelt worden, das heißt für Lernende mit sonderpädagogischem Förderbedarf, die zieldifferent unterrichtet werden.

food – word bank

fruits	Obst/Früchte
apple	Apfel
banana	Banane
cherry	Kirsche
peach	Pfirsich
pineapple	Ananas
orange	Orange
pear	Birne
grape	Weintraube
kiwi	Kiwi
plum	Pflaume
fruit salad	Obstsalat

vegetables	Gemüse
tomato/tomatoes	Tomate/Tomaten
cucumber	Gurke
potato/potatoes	Kartoffel/Kartoffeln
lettuce	Blattsalat
onion	Zwiebel
carrot	Karotte
pea	Erbse
bean	Bohne
spinach	Spinat

food – word bank

drinks	Getränke
water	Wasser
milk	Milch
tea	Tee
coffee	Kaffee
(orange) juice	(Orangen-)Saft
sugary drinks	Süßgetränke

food	Lebensmittel
pizza	Pizza
fish	Fisch
meat	Fleisch
burger	Burger
sandwich	Sandwich, belegtes Brot
soup	Suppe
cheese	Käse
bread	Brot
salad	Salat
cake	Kuchen
sweets	Süßigkeiten
biscuits	Gebäck, Kekse
rice	Reis
grain	Getreide

food – word bank

meals	Mahlzeiten
breakfast	Frühstück
lunch	Mittagessen
dinner	Abendessen
menu	Speisekarte
starter	Vorspeise
main dish	Hauptspeise
dessert	Dessert, Nachspeise

dishes	Geschirr
cutlery	Besteck
knife	Messer
fork	Gabel
spoon	Löffel
plate	Teller
glass	Glas
bowl	Schale, Schüssel

food at the market and in the restaurant 1

① **Find the food words.**

L	J	I	Z	N	U	P	M	G	D	S	Q	H	Z	E	M	F	U
A	S	O	U	P	R	X	V	H	P	T	E	A	L	S	E	S	Y
Z	K	N	I	F	E	C	P	L	U	M	H	X	K	T	I	H	K
X	C	Q	E	R	C	K	G	X	R	F	F	I	S	H	M	M	P
R	L	U	G	O	J	Z	H	I	B	J	P	D	J	Q	Q	W	N
O	C	M	H	B	L	M	P	C	J	C	O	F	F	E	E	L	M
D	B	H	M	H	G	L	E	A	E	J	L	L	X	F	P	E	A
W	R	W	Y	U	O	F	A	X	E	B	F	H	B	Q	W	E	Q
W	E	G	N	D	K	O	R	V	Y	D	J	A	L	M	F	B	O
H	A	Y	N	G	H	R	V	X	N	R	Y	K	E	V	Q	E	N
R	D	J	H	H	Y	K	G	Q	R	T	K	B	T	U	R	A	I
C	U	T	L	E	R	Y	O	J	T	Q	I	K	T	X	D	N	O
S	Y	J	U	M	N	Y	V	R	B	K	W	V	U	R	F	X	N
W	X	E	F	Q	R	R	P	I	M	M	I	T	C	F	G	D	U
E	P	I	Z	Z	A	I	Y	H	J	J	W	T	E	B	D	J	Y
E	Y	K	K	E	P	O	X	B	E	N	I	O	P	M	A	X	H
T	H	M	F	Z	V	E	K	H	O	F	K	C	X	Z	F	L	H
S	W	S	E	M	T	U	M	W	A	T	E	R	K	Q	T	T	W

② **Cross out the odd word.**

1. lunch, coffee, dinner, breakfast
2. sweets, chocolate, fish, cake
3. water, milk, meat, juice
4. salad, fruit, bread, vegetable
5. fork, spoon, plate, lunch
6. tomato, plum, cherry, apple

food at the market and in the restaurant 2

③ **Crossword puzzle**

Fill in the English words.

1. Getränk
2. Wasser
3. Zwiebel
4. Gurke
5. Kirsche
6. Apfel
7. Ananas
8. Tomate
9. Banane
10. Blattsalat
11. Kartoffel
12. Karotte
13. Käse
14. Milch
15. Brot
16. Kuchen
17. Speisekarte
18. Fleisch
19. Birne
20. Pfirsich

food at the market and in the restaurant 3

④ **Mediation**

You are in London with a friend. She doesn't speak English and she wants to know what her sentences and questions mean.

Translate.

1. Ich habe Hunger.

2. Ich esse kein Fleisch.

3. Ich habe Durst. Was gibt es zu trinken?

4. Gibt es Pizza?

5. Was können wir bestellen?

6. Können wir das Essen mitnehmen oder müssen wir hier essen?

7. Ich trinke nur Wasser.

8. Das ist sehr lecker.

9. Das Menü ist sehr teuer.

10. Das ist mein Lieblingsgericht.

food at the market and in the restaurant 1

❶ **Find as many words as you can in the word puzzle and colour them.**

Finde möglichst viele Begriffe in diesem Suchsel und markiere sie farbig. Die fettgedruckten Anfangsbuchstaben helfen dir.

L	J	I	Z	N	U	P	M	G	D	S	Q	H	Z	E	M	F	U
A	**S**	O	U	P	R	X	V	H	P	**T**	E	A	L	S	E	S	Y
Z	**K**	N	I	F	E	C	**P**	L	U	M	H	X	K	T	I	H	K
X	C	Q	E	R	C	K	G	X	R	**F**	I	S	H	M	M	P
R	L	U	G	O	J	Z	H	I	B	J	P	D	J	Q	Q	W	N
O	C	M	H	B	L	M	**P**	C	J	**C**	O	F	F	E	E	L	M
D	**B**	H	M	H	G	L	E	A	E	J	L	L	X	F	**P**	E	A
W	R	W	Y	U	O	**F**	A	X	E	B	F	H	B	Q	W	E	Q
W	E	G	N	D	K	O	R	V	Y	D	J	A	**L**	M	F	**B**	O
H	A	Y	N	G	H	R	V	X	N	R	Y	K	E	V	Q	E	N
R	D	J	H	H	Y	K	G	Q	R	T	**K**	B	T	U	R	A	I
C	U	T	L	E	R	Y	O	J	T	Q	I	K	T	X	D	N	O
S	Y	J	U	M	N	Y	V	R	B	K	W	V	U	R	F	X	N
W	X	E	F	Q	R	R	P	I	M	M	I	T	C	F	G	D	U
E	**P**	I	Z	Z	A	I	Y	H	J	J	W	T	E	B	D	J	Y
E	Y	K	K	E	P	O	X	B	E	N	I	O	P	M	A	X	H
T	H	M	F	Z	V	E	K	H	O	F	K	C	X	Z	F	L	H
S	W	S	E	M	T	U	M	**W**	A	T	E	R	K	Q	T	W

❷ **Cross out the odd word.**

Streiche das falsche Wort durch.

1. lunch, **c**offee, dinner, breakfast
2. sweets, chocolate, **f**ish, cake
3. water, milk, **m**eat, juice
4. salad, fruit, **b**read, vegetable
5. fork, spoon, plate, **l**unch

food at the market and in the restaurant 2

3 Crossword puzzle

Find the English words in this crossword puzzle.

Löse das Kreuzworträtsel. Die Anfangsbuchstaben der gesuchten Wörter sind schon vorgegeben.

1. Getränk
2. Wasser
3. Zwiebel
4. Gurke
5. Kirsche
6. Apfel
7. Ananas
8. Tomate
9. Banane
10. Blattsalat
11. Kartoffel
12. Karotte
13. Käse
14. Milch
15. Brot
16. Kuchen
17. Speisekarte
18. Fleisch
19. Birne
20. Pfirsich

food at the market and in the restaurant 3

❹ Mediation

You are in London with a friend.
She doesn't speak English and she wants to know what her sentences and questions mean.

Connect the right sentences and write the pairs in the table.

Du bist mit einer Freundin in London.
Sie spricht kein Englisch, aber sie möchte wissen, was ihre Sätze und Fragen auf Englisch bedeuten.

Verbinde die Sätze richtig und trage sie passend in die Tabelle ein.

① Ich habe Hunger.

② Ich esse kein Fleisch.

③ Ich habe Durst. Was gibt es zu trinken?

④ Gibt es Pizza?

⑤ Was können wir bestellen?

⑥ Können wir das Essen mitnehmen oder müssen wir hier essen?

⑦ Ich trinke nur Wasser.

Ⓐ Can we take the food with us or do we have to eat here?

Ⓑ I am thirsty. What is there to drink?

Ⓒ What can we order?

Ⓓ I am hungry.

Ⓔ I only drink water.

Ⓕ Do they have pizza?

Ⓖ I don't eat meat.

1	2	3	4	5	6	7

healthy and unhealthy food 1

① What is healthy and what is unhealthy?
Fill in the chart. How many words do you know?

healthy food	unhealthy food

② Write down healthy and unhealthy things to do.
Look at the example and find more things.

healthy things to do	unhealthy things to do
drink water	*drink sugary drinks*

healthy and unhealthy food 2

③ **Food pyramid**

Look at the foods and drinks in the pyramid. Take the second pyramid and write down all of the names you know. Use a dictionary or the internet to find out the words you don't know.

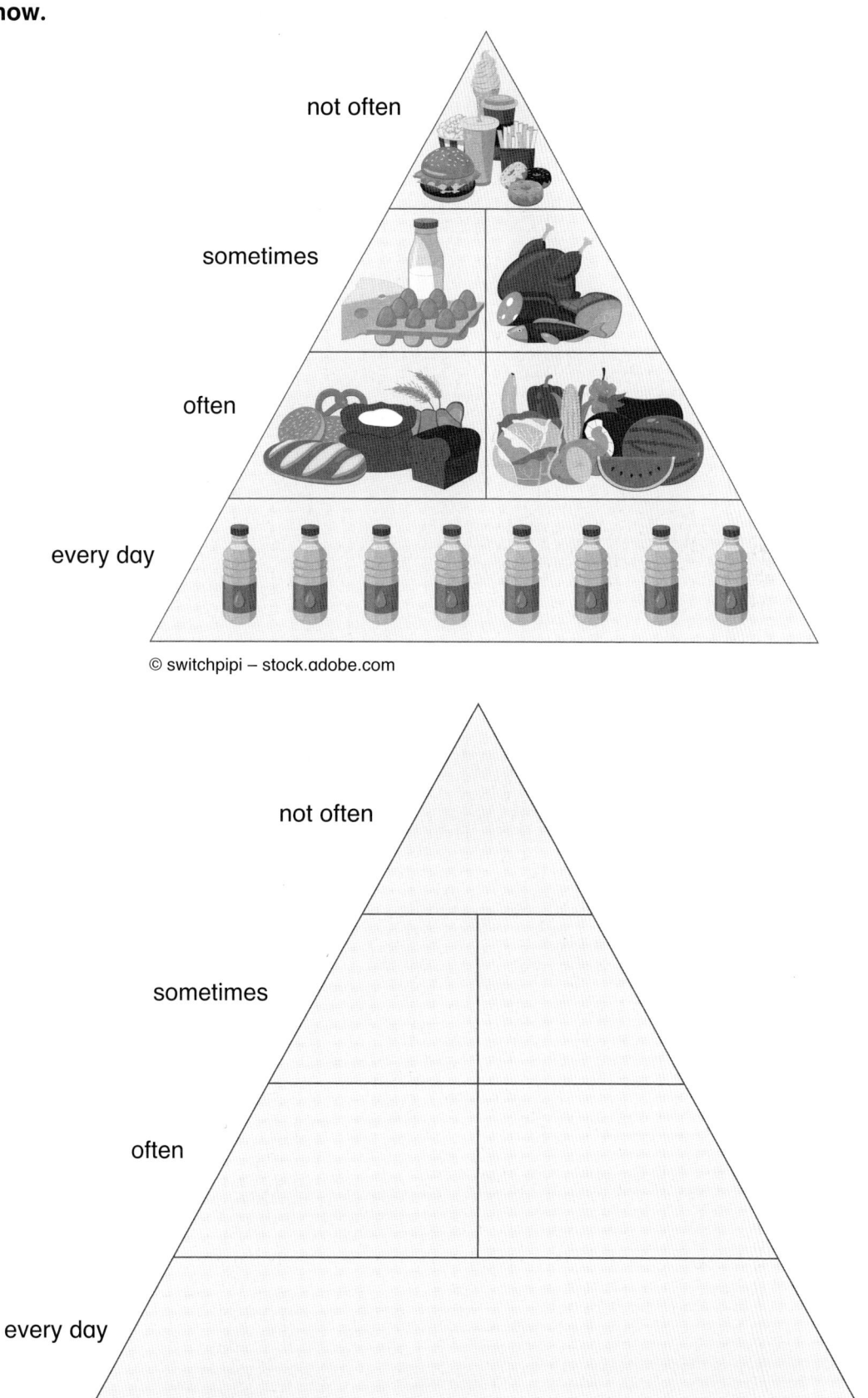

© switchpipi – stock.adobe.com

© switchpipi – stock.adobe.com

healthy and unhealthy food 3

④ **Food diary**

Write down the food and drinks that you have eaten and drunk often, sometimes or not at all this week.

	no	some	a lot of
Monday			
Tuesday			
Wednesday			
Thursday			
Friday			
Saturday			
Sunday			

⑤ **Fill in this chart. What do you eat …**

… before school?	… at school?	… after school?	… at the weekend?

healthy and unhealthy food 1

❶ Which food and drinks are healthy and what is unhealthy?
Fill in the chart with the words from the box.

Was ist gesund und was ist ungesund?
Vervollständige die Tabelle mit den Begriffen aus der Box.

> cake • meat • cheese • sweets • fish • pizza • potatoes • salad • oranges • banana • coke • water • biscuits • chocolate • ice cream • pudding

healthy	unhealthy

healthy and unhealthy food 2

❷ **What are healthy and unhealthy things to do? Tick the right answers.**

Was ist gesund und was ist ungesund? Kreuze die richtigen Aussagen an.

	healthy things to do	unhealthy things to do
to do sport	☐	☐
to walk whenever you can	☐	☐
to smoke	☐	☐
to eat fruits and vegetables	☐	☐
to eat too much sugar and fat	☐	☐
to use too much soap	☐	☐
to wash your hands	☐	☐
to get plenty of sleep	☐	☐
to go to bed late	☐	☐

❸ **Food pyramid**

Look at the foods and drinks in the pyramid and write down the names.

Schau dir die Ernährungspyramide an und ordne die Begriffe den entsprechenden Stufen zu.

> bread • burger • cheese • chicken • coffee • eggs • fish • fries • fruits • grain • ice cream • meat • milk • sausages • sweets • vegetables • water

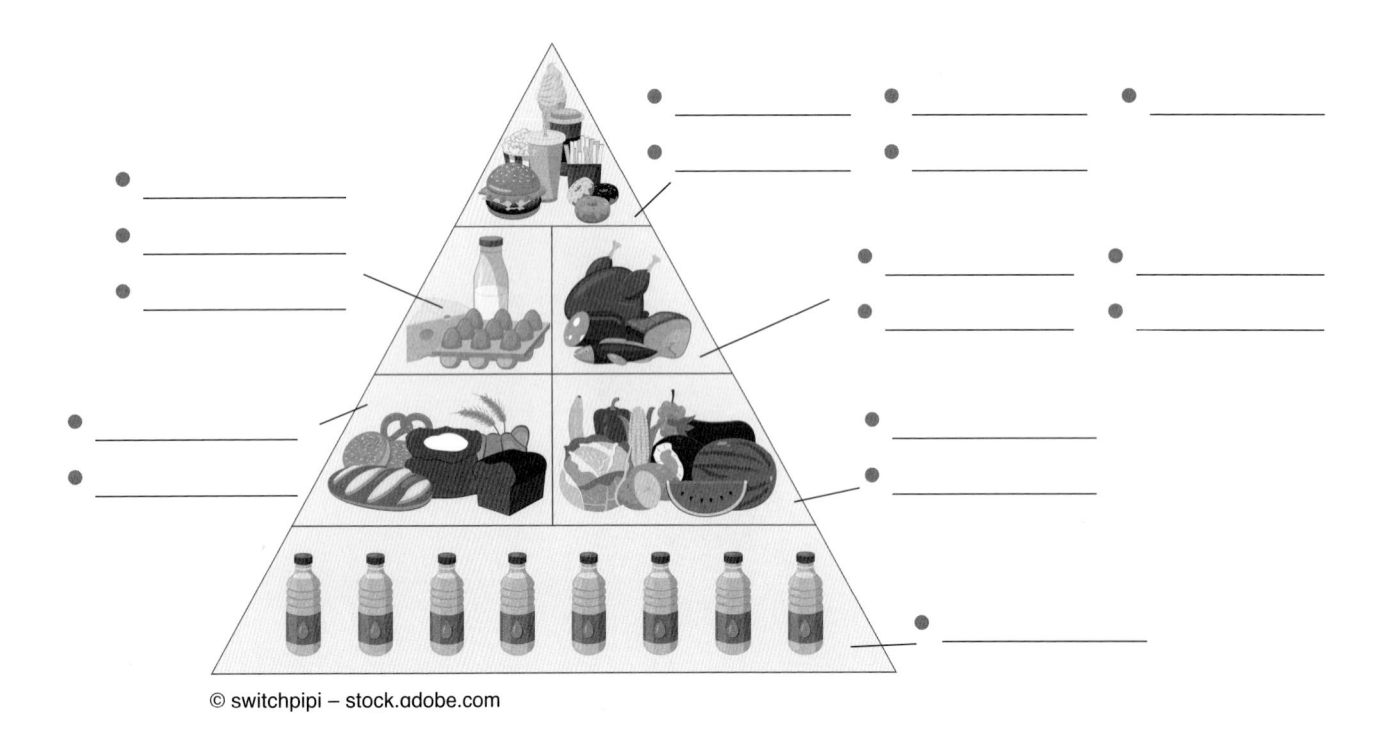

© switchpipi – stock.adobe.com

healthy and unhealthy food 3

❹ Write a food diary. What did you eat and drink this week?
Have a look at the words in the box.

Schreibe ein Ernährungstagebuch: Was hast du diese Woche oft, manchmal oder gar nicht gegessen und getrunken?

Die Begriffe in der Box helfen dir.

> ice tea • water • bread • chips • chocolate • fruits • vegetables • bread • cheese

	no (kein)	some (ein wenig)	a lot of (eine Menge)
Monday			
Tuesday			
Wednesday			
Thursday			
Friday			
Saturday			
Sunday			

❺ What do you eat … Fill in this chart.
Use the words from the word bank as help.

Was isst du vor, in und nach der Schule und am Wochenende?

Trage in die Tabelle ein.
Du kannst die Wörter aus der *word bank* zu Hilfe nehmen.

… before school?	… at school?	… after school?	… at the weekend?

guessing game

Try to explain these words to your group. You are not allowed to use the words below.

MILK white cow fridge	**APPLE** healthy red green
CHEESE yellow bread fridge	**BANANA** monkey yellow fruit
CUCUMBER vegetable green salad	**BREAD** breakfast oven brown
CAKE birthday candle sweet	**MEAT** vegetarian animal pig

guessing game

MENU	SWEETS
restaurant	children
choose	unhealthy
food	sugar

WATER	CHERRY
drink	fruit
bottle	red
healthy	tree

TOMATO	CARROT
red	orange
vegetable	rabbit
salad	vegetable

1 guessing game

Try to explain these words to your group.
You can use the words below.

Erkläre die Begriffe deiner Gruppe.
Du kannst dazu die Wörter unter den Begriffen verwenden.

MILK	APPLE
white cow fridge	healthy red green
CHEESE	BANANA
yellow bread fridge	monkey yellow fruit
CUCUMBER	BREAD
vegetable green salad	breakfast oven brown

guessing game

CAKE birthday candle sweet	**MEAT** vegetarian animal pig
MENU restaurant choose food	**SWEETS** children unhealthy sugar
WATER drink bottle healthy	**CHERRY** fruit red tree
TOMATO red vegetable salad	**CARROT** orange rabbit vegetable

2 school holidays – word bank

countries and continents	Länder und Kontinente
GB – Great Britain	Großbritannien
Germany	Deutschland
Australia	Australien
USA – United States of America	USA – Die vereinigten Staaten von Amerika
Africa	Afrika
France	Frankreich
Portugal	Portugal
Denmark	Dänemark
Austria	Österreich
Switzerland	Schweiz
Italy	Italien
Poland	Polen
Russia	Russland
Spain	Spanien
Netherlands	Holland / Niederlande
Turkey	Türkei

languages	Sprachen
English	Englisch
German	Deutsch
Turkish	Türkisch
Italian	Italienisch
Polish	Polnisch
Spanish	Spanisch
Russian	Russisch
French	Französisch

school holidays – word bank

holiday activities	Ferienaktivitäten
(to) go on a holiday	in den Urlaub fahren
(to) have a holiday	Urlaub / Ferien haben
(to) go abroad	verreisen (ins Ausland)
(to) travel	reisen
(to) stay at home	zu Hause bleiben
(to) go / travel by car, plane, train …	mit dem Auto, Flugzeug, Zug … verreisen
(to) take the bus, train, car	den Bus, den Zug, das Auto nehmen
(to) fly to Spain	nach Spanien fliegen
(to) do something outside	etwas draußen unternehmen
(to) swim in the sea	im Meer schwimmen
(to) lie on the beach	am Strand liegen
(to) walk along the beach	am Strand spazieren
(to) enjoy the sunshine	die Sonne genießen
(to) relax	sich entspannen, erholen
(to) eat at a restaurant	in einem Restaurant essen
(to) take photos	Bilder machen, fotografieren
(to) do sightseeing	Sehenswürdigkeiten besichtigen
(to) hang out with friends	mit Freunden abhängen
(to) sleep over at a friend's house	bei einem Freund / Freundin übernachten
(to) stay in a hotel	in einem Hotel übernachten
(to) meet someone on holiday	jdn. im Urlaub kennenlernen
(to) go swimming	schwimmen gehen
(to) go on a bike ride	eine Fahrradtour machen
(to) go to a camp	zu einem Camp fahren
(to) go on a boat trip	eine Bootstour machen
(to) go to an adventure park	in einen Abenteuerpark gehen
(to) go to a holiday park	zu einem Ferienpark fahren
(to) go shopping	shoppen gehen
(to) go on a sightseeing tour	eine Sightseeingtour machen
(to) go to the zoo	in den Zoo gehen
(to) buy souvenirs	Souvenirs kaufen
(to) write a postcard	eine Postkarte schreiben
tourist attraction	Touristenattraktion

school holidays – word bank

places and attractions	Orte und Attraktionen
coffee shop	Café
museum	Museum
souvenir shop	Souvenirladen
tower	Turm
bridge	Brücke
castle	Burg, Schloss
palace	Palast
mosque	Moschee
at a museum	in einem Museum
at the beach	am Strand
in the countryside	auf dem Land
in the mountains	in den Bergen
at the seaside	am (Strand-)Ufer
ticket price	Eintrittsgeld, Ticketpreis
opening hours	Öffnungszeiten
(to) buy a ticket for	ein Ticket kaufen für

school holidays – countries and activities 1

① **Find the countries, continents and languages. There are 16 words that you should find.**

P	L	X	E	F	W	O	P	R	R	C	C	M	F	I	U	G	A	V	A	W	I
I	I	O	R	L	G	E	R	M	A	N	G	E	G	V	D	Z	Y	T	U	R	G
P	H	M	E	K	L	Z	O	D	S	K	N	R	P	P	P	P	F	J	I	S	P	F
L	O	T	U	R	K	I	S	H	G	B	C	U	S	R	G	B	S	V	T	D	C
Q	U	E	N	P	O	L	I	S	H	V	A	S	D	X	J	Q	W	R	R	L	A
G	P	E	F	M	X	Y	A	X	J	T	Y	S	S	F	Q	H	I	O	A	P	H
I	I	E	V	X	G	W	T	H	B	G	W	I	E	J	B	A	T	F	L	C	O
R	R	L	I	X	F	J	U	R	Q	S	Y	A	I	E	I	D	Z	I	I	A	K
Q	R	H	W	O	P	B	Y	L	R	A	F	N	T	Y	H	K	E	T	A	F	R
D	R	D	Y	H	R	N	X	A	A	N	E	G	A	I	K	S	R	A	I	R	H
I	O	F	T	V	F	E	N	R	F	N	T	D	L	E	L	Q	L	L	X	I	P
Y	M	R	Q	R	Q	T	E	P	K	D	B	V	I	Y	M	C	A	Y	V	C	Q
R	P	E	Q	U	V	H	E	N	Y	D	J	B	A	D	O	C	N	V	Y	A	S
V	K	N	V	S	U	E	F	V	X	M	J	Y	N	R	C	Y	D	F	C	F	I
U	R	C	J	A	K	R	C	N	I	F	R	A	N	C	E	Y	V	O	X	S	K
J	N	H	V	E	S	L	X	U	W	B	L	W	X	C	J	S	N	Z	Q	P	X
T	W	V	O	B	S	A	Q	D	E	N	M	A	R	K	R	O	G	V	J	K	W
A	A	A	R	I	V	N	F	C	T	X	U	G	E	R	M	A	N	Y	U	U	M
F	A	M	J	J	W	D	P	N	J	U	Q	Y	E	H	W	W	V	P	R	G	X
K	U	W	U	D	A	S	N	Z	H	O	U	U	B	A	H	H	D	P	A	V	K
Q	C	S	O	S	G	R	E	A	T	B	R	I	T	A	I	N	V	U	K	K	S
S	J	W	S	I	R	E	O	O	Z	J	N	V	H	H	W	R	P	K	D	C	D

country	continent	language

school holidays – countries and activities 2

② **Find the holiday activities, places and attractions. There are 15 words that you should find.**

H	S	F	A	W	S	P	G	I	I	B	F	C	P	L	N	Y	J	F	Y	X	W	H
S	R	S	X	Z	M	W	O	N	F	V	P	E	N	W	K	D	W	S	G	Y	H	N
O	X	B	Y	S	K	O	F	D	M	B	N	U	J	J	I	M	A	P	O	B	B	R
J	P	V	I	W	C	M	M	J	X	P	W	T	K	I	Y	P	H	Y	A	R	U	B
L	X	X	L	G	H	M	S	L	S	M	B	I	S	R	E	L	A	X	B	E	Y	D
W	E	F	R	O	E	B	L	U	G	S	J	W	X	Q	Y	F	H	G	R	B	R	L
U	H	X	Z	X	M	T	A	E	L	G	Y	Q	Y	T	B	Y	W	G	O	E	M	H
V	V	V	X	Y	X	U	F	I	F	T	S	P	A	L	A	C	E	U	A	E	M	D
R	F	Q	E	W	R	I	T	E	A	P	O	S	T	C	A	R	D	P	D	V	W	H
M	W	N	M	O	O	L	Q	R	M	V	D	H	B	V	S	C	G	H	T	I	R	V
O	U	D	B	R	S	B	I	M	Q	C	P	X	R	G	U	A	V	F	U	G	O	I
S	Q	S	O	W	S	H	J	D	I	X	G	N	I	V	D	S	C	C	T	O	C	L
Q	S	X	P	Y	P	R	E	Q	F	W	S	R	D	O	R	T	N	R	T	P	O	O
U	M	M	T	M	W	M	N	G	M	F	O	I	G	S	K	L	D	G	R	E	F	M
E	S	O	U	V	E	N	I	R	S	H	O	P	E	V	G	E	N	P	A	N	F	K
Y	M	T	O	U	R	I	S	T	A	T	T	R	A	C	T	I	O	N	V	I	E	B
E	B	O	Y	C	M	I	Q	T	T	O	D	C	M	V	B	U	K	W	E	N	E	J
R	Y	B	S	Q	H	F	L	P	Q	T	N	Q	Z	M	J	T	P	X	L	G	S	R
B	X	G	B	U	O	B	E	U	S	I	G	H	T	S	E	E	I	N	G	H	H	B
N	N	I	O	M	Q	T	E	O	I	F	F	F	T	T	Q	I	P	F	O	O	O	X
X	O	Y	W	U	X	W	T	I	C	K	E	T	P	R	I	C	E	V	B	U	P	I
D	A	D	H	T	O	W	E	R	M	C	X	A	Z	T	X	L	H	O	C	R	K	R
W	Q	J	W	V	Y	I	Q	G	T	N	J	L	S	P	V	F	B	S	B	S	D	G

school holidays – countries and activities 3

③ Fill in this mind map with words that you remember from your last summer holidays. Think about activities you did and places you visited.

_____

_____

_____   _____

_____   _____

_____   (my holidays)   _____

_____   _____

_____   _____

④ Now write a text about your last summer holidays. Write about 60 words and use the ideas from the mind map. Don't forget to use the simple past.

MY SUMMER HOLIDAYS

_____

_____

_____

_____

_____

_____

_____

_____

_____

school holidays – countries and activities 4

⑤ **At the beach**

Hi, I'm Luca and I am at the beach in Italy with my family. It's great here and we have a lot of fun. Yesterday we visited an old castle. That was really cool but my brother lost his camera with all of the great pictures. Our hotel is also great and the rooms are very big. I love the Italian food, especially the ice cream. My mother always says that I should stop eating so much ice cream. She is afraid that I get stomach aches and then we have to go to the doctor. But I think it's holiday time and I can eat as much as I want. At the beach I met some nice boys. We play together and enjoy the sunshine. I love summer holidays and I hope we will come back soon.

Answer these questions in complete sentences:

1. Where is Luca and who is with him?

   _____

2. What did he visit yesterday?

   _____

3. What got lost?

   _____

4. What does Luca like best?

   _____

5. What does he enjoy?

   _____

2 school holidays – countries and activities 5

⑥ **One summer day but different activities!**
Look at the pictures and write down what the people are doing.

1. _____

2. _____

3. _____

4. _____

5. _____

6. _____

school holidays – countries and activities 6

⑦ **My town is a fantastic place**

Write a blog entry for tourists coming to your town (100 words). They need ideas for great places.

Include the following aspects, and write down your blog.

> *What do you like about your village / hometown?*
> *What is special about it?*
> *What is your favourite place? What must be visited by tourists and why?*
> *Where do you go shopping? Are there special restaurants?*
> *What activities can you do in your town?*

MY TOWN IS A FANTASTIC PLACE

© Mariia – stock.adobe.com

school holidays – countries and activities 1

❶ Find as many words about countries, continents and languages as you can in the word puzzle and colour them.

Finde möglichst viele Begriffe zu Ländern, Kontinenten und Sprachen in diesem Suchsel und markiere sie farbig.

Die fettgedruckten Anfangsbuchstaben helfen dir.

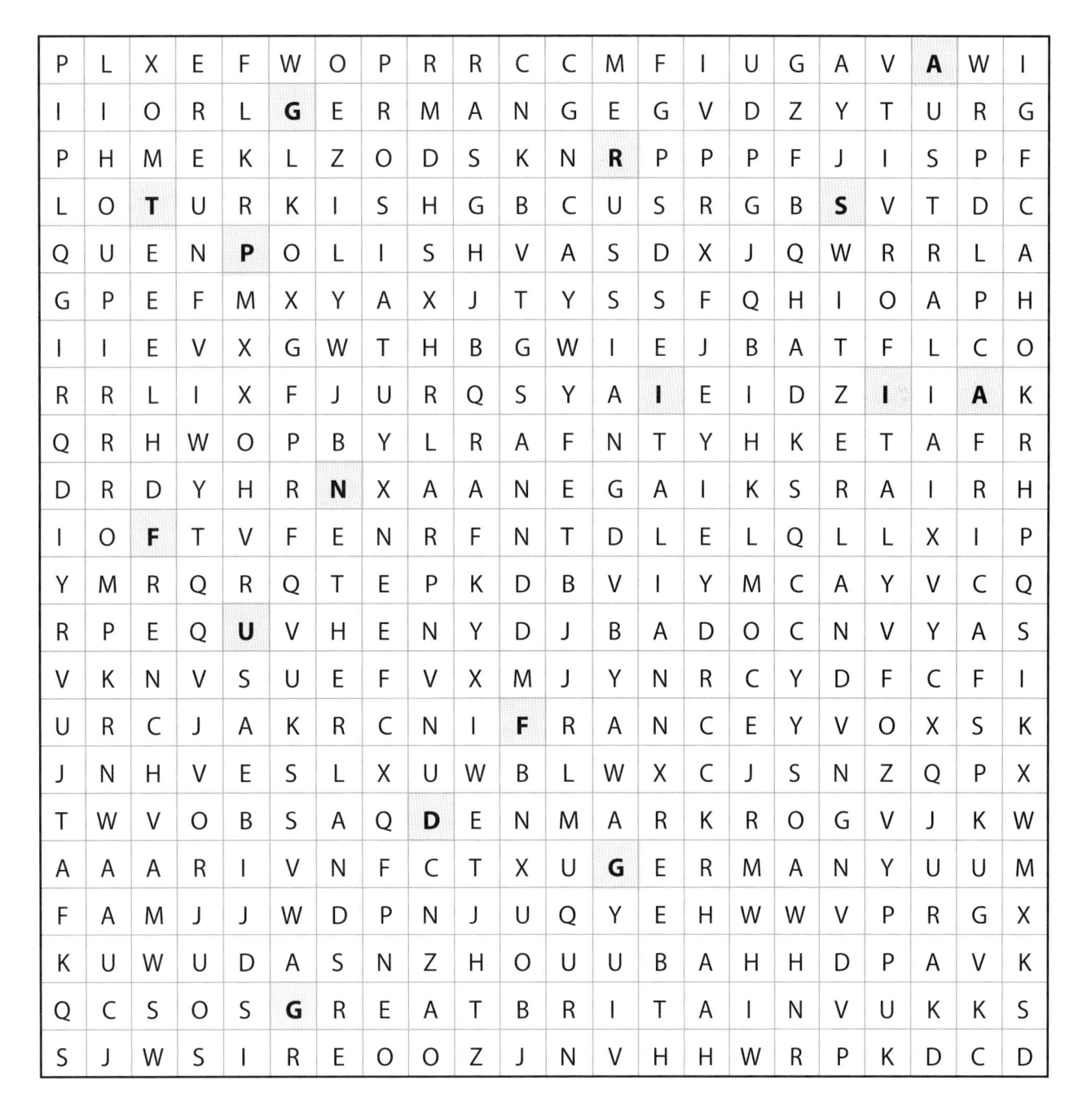

P	L	X	E	F	W	O	P	R	R	C	C	M	F	I	U	G	A	V	**A**	W	I
I	I	O	R	L	**G**	E	R	M	A	N	G	E	G	V	D	Z	Y	T	U	R	G
P	H	M	E	K	L	Z	O	D	S	K	N	**R**	P	P	P	F	J	I	S	P	F
L	O	**T**	U	R	K	I	S	H	G	B	C	U	S	R	G	B	**S**	V	T	D	C
Q	U	E	N	**P**	O	L	I	S	H	V	A	S	D	X	J	Q	W	R	R	L	A
G	P	E	F	M	X	Y	A	X	J	T	Y	S	S	F	Q	H	I	O	A	P	H
I	I	E	V	X	G	W	T	H	B	G	W	I	E	J	B	A	T	F	L	C	O
R	R	L	I	X	F	J	U	R	Q	S	Y	A	**I**	E	I	D	Z	**I**	I	**A**	K
Q	R	H	W	O	P	B	Y	L	R	A	F	N	T	Y	H	K	E	T	A	F	R
D	R	D	Y	H	R	**N**	X	A	A	N	E	G	A	I	K	S	R	A	I	R	H
I	O	**F**	T	V	F	E	N	R	F	N	T	D	L	E	L	Q	L	L	X	I	P
Y	M	R	Q	R	Q	T	E	P	K	D	B	V	I	Y	M	C	A	Y	V	C	Q
R	P	E	Q	**U**	V	H	E	N	Y	D	J	B	A	D	O	C	N	V	Y	A	S
V	K	N	V	S	U	E	F	V	X	M	J	Y	N	R	C	Y	D	F	C	F	I
U	R	C	J	A	K	R	C	N	I	**F**	R	A	N	C	E	Y	V	O	X	S	K
J	N	H	V	E	S	L	X	U	W	B	L	W	X	C	J	S	N	Z	Q	P	X
T	W	V	O	B	S	A	Q	**D**	E	N	M	A	R	K	R	O	G	V	J	K	W
A	A	A	R	I	V	N	F	C	T	X	U	**G**	E	R	M	A	N	Y	U	U	M
F	A	M	J	J	W	D	P	N	J	U	Q	Y	E	H	W	W	W	V	P	R	G	X
K	U	W	U	D	A	S	N	Z	H	O	U	U	B	A	H	H	D	P	A	V	K
Q	C	S	O	S	**G**	R	E	A	T	B	R	I	T	A	I	N	V	U	K	K	S
S	J	W	S	I	R	E	O	O	Z	J	N	V	H	H	W	R	P	K	D	C	D

school holidays – countries and activities 2

❷ **Find as many words about holiday activities, places and attractions as you can in the word puzzle and colour them.**

Finde möglichst viele Begriffe über Ferienaktivitäten, Orte und Attraktionen in diesem Suchsel und markiere sie farbig.

Die fettgedruckten Anfangsbuchstaben helfen dir.

H	S	F	A	W	S	P	G	I	I	B	F	C	P	L	N	Y	J	F	Y	X	W	H
S	R	S	X	Z	M	W	O	N	F	V	P	E	N	W	K	D	W	S	**G**	Y	H	N
O	X	B	Y	S	K	O	F	D	M	B	N	U	J	J	I	M	A	P	O	B	B	R
J	P	V	I	W	C	M	M	J	X	P	W	T	K	I	Y	P	H	Y	A	R	U	B
L	X	X	L	G	H	M	S	L	S	M	B	I	S	**R**	E	L	A	X	B	E	Y	D
W	E	F	R	O	E	B	L	U	G	S	J	W	X	Q	Y	F	H	G	R	B	R	L
U	H	X	Z	X	M	T	A	E	L	G	Y	Q	Y	T	B	Y	W	G	O	E	M	H
V	V	V	X	Y	X	U	F	I	F	T	S	**P**	A	L	A	C	E	U	A	E	M	D
R	F	Q	E	**W**	R	I	T	E	A	P	O	S	T	C	A	R	D	P	D	V	W	H
M	W	N	M	O	O	L	Q	R	M	V	D	H	**B**	V	S	**C**	G	H	T	I	R	V
O	U	D	B	R	S	B	I	M	Q	C	P	X	R	G	U	A	V	F	U	G	O	I
S	Q	S	O	W	S	H	J	D	I	X	G	N	I	V	D	S	C	C	T	**O**	**C**	L
Q	S	X	P	Y	P	R	E	Q	F	W	S	R	D	O	R	T	N	R	**T**	P	O	O
U	M	M	T	M	W	M	N	G	M	F	O	I	G	S	K	L	D	G	R	E	F	M
E	**S**	O	U	V	E	N	I	R	S	H	O	P	E	V	G	E	N	P	A	N	F	K
Y	M	**T**	O	U	R	I	S	T	A	T	T	R	A	C	T	I	O	N	V	I	E	B
E	B	O	Y	C	M	I	Q	T	T	O	D	C	M	V	B	U	K	W	E	N	E	J
R	Y	B	S	Q	H	F	L	P	Q	T	N	Q	Z	M	J	T	P	X	L	G	S	R
B	X	G	B	U	O	B	E	U	**S**	I	G	H	T	S	E	E	I	N	G	H	H	B
N	N	I	O	M	Q	T	E	O	I	F	F	F	T	T	Q	I	P	F	O	O	O	X
X	O	Y	W	U	X	W	**T**	I	C	K	E	T	P	R	I	C	E	V	B	U	P	I
D	A	D	H	**T**	O	W	E	R	M	C	X	A	Z	T	X	L	H	O	C	R	K	R
W	Q	J	W	V	Y	I	Q	G	T	N	J	L	S	P	V	F	B	S	B	S	D	G

school holidays – countries and activities 3

❸ Fill in this mind map with words that you remember from your last summer holidays. Think about activities you did and places you visited.

Befülle die Mindmap mit Begriffen aus deinem letzten Sommerurlaub. Überlege dir, an welchen Orten du warst und was du gemacht hast.

a) activities   MY HOLIDAYS   b) places

_____   _____

_____   _____

_____   _____

_____   _____

❹ Now write a text about your last summer holidays.

Write about 40 words and use the ideas from your mind map. Don't forget to use the simple past. You can also use the ideas and verbs in the box or the picture.

Verfasse einen Text über deinen letzten Sommerurlaub. Schreibe 40 Wörter und verwende die Ideen aus deiner Mindmap. Vergiss nicht, das Simple Past als Zeitform zu verwenden. Du kannst auch die Ideen und Verben aus der Box nutzen und dich von dem Bild inspirieren lassen.

stayed	in a hotel
swam	in the sea
ate	ice cream
met	nice people
enjoyed	beautiful sights

MY SUMMER HOLIDAYS

_____

_____

_____

_____

school holidays – countries and activities 4

5 At the beach

Hi, I'm Luca and I am **at the beach in Italy with my family**. It's great here and we have a lot of fun. Yesterday we visited **an old castle**. That was really cool but my brother **lost his camera** with all of the great pictures. Our hotel is also great and the rooms are very big. I love the Italian food, especially the **ice cream**. My mother always says that I should stop eating so much ice cream. She is afraid that I get stomach aches and then we have to go the doctor. But I think it's holiday time and I can eat as much as I want. At the beach I met some nice boys. We play together and **enjoy the sunshine**. I love summer holidays and I hope we are coming back soon.

Answer these questions in complete sentences.
Beantworte die Fragen in vollständigen Sätzen.

1. Where is Luca and who is with him?

2. What did he visit yesterday?

3. What got lost?

4. What does he like best?

5. What does Luca enjoy?

---

especially = besonders

stomach aches = Bauchschmerzen

school holidays – countries and activities 5

6 One summer day but different activities!
Look at the pictures and connect them with the right sentences.

Schau dir die Bilder an und verbinde sie mit den passenden Sätzen.

	The boy is going on a bike ride.
	The man is relaxing / enjoying the sunshine.
	The family is watching the sea lions at the zoo.
	The man and the boy are walking along the beach.
	The family is having a picnic.
	The friends are eating ice cream.

school holidays – countries and activities 6

❼ My town is a fantastic place

Write a blog entry for tourists coming to your town.
They need ideas for great places (60 words).
Use the ideas in the box.

Schreibe einen Blog-Eintrag über deine Stadt für Besucher und Touristen.
Sie brauchen Ideen und Tipps für schöne Orte (60 Wörter).
Beachte auch die Fragen in der Box.

What do you like about your village / hometown?
What is special about it?
What is your favourite place?
Where do you go shopping?
What activities can you do in your town?

MY TOWN IS A FANTASTIC PLACE

Hello everybody,

today I am writing about my town and why tourists should visit it.

I love my town because …

© Mariia – stock.adobe.com

3 my school day – word bank

at school	in der Schule
school start	Schulanfang
term	Trimester *(das engl. Schuljahr wird in 3 Abschnitte = Trimester eingeteilt)*
assembly	Versammlung
education	Erziehung, Schulbildung
locker	Schließfach
timetable	Stundenplan
meeting	Treffen, Besprechung
registration	Registrierung, Erfassung
principal	Schuldirektor, Schuldirektorin
teacher	Lehrer, Lehrerin
caretaker	Hausmeister
(to) teach	unterrichten
(to) work	arbeiten
school rules	Schulregeln
break	Pause

school uniform	Schuluniform
blazer	Blazer
tie	Krawatte
skirt	Rock
blouse	Bluse
shirt	Hemd
trousers	Hose
shorts	kurze Hose
shoes	Schuhe

TIMETABLE

⏲	Monday	Tuesday	Wednesday	Thursday	Friday

my school day – word bank

What's in your school bag?	Was ist in deiner Schultasche?
school bag	Schultasche
book	Buch
exercise book	Übungsheft
pencil case	Etui, Federmäppchen
sharpener	Anspitzer
rubber	Radiergummi
pencil	Bleistift
ruler	Lineal
felt-tip (pen)	Filzstift
pen	Füller
coloured pencil	Buntstift
folder	Mappe
scissors	Schere
calculator	Taschenrechner
hole punch	Locher

rooms and places at school	Zimmer und Orte in der Schule
canteen	Kantine
classroom	Klassenzimmer
assembly hall	Aula
schoolyard	Schulhof
sports hall	Sporthalle
science lab	Chemieraum
drama room	Theaterraum

my school day – word bank

school subjects	Schulfächer
subject	Fach
English	Englisch
German	Deutsch
French	Französisch
maths	Mathematik
geography	Erdkunde, Geografie
technology	Technik
history	Geschichte
art	Kunst
science	Naturwissenschaften
chemistry	Chemie
biology	Biologie
PE (Physical Education)	Sport
RE (Religious Education)	Religion
drama	Literaturkurs, Theater-AG
ICT (Information Computer Technology)	Informatik

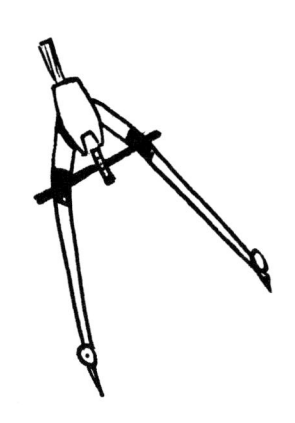

my school day 1

① **Crossword puzzles**

Fill in the missing words.

1. Versammlung
2. Erziehung, Schulbildung
3. Stundenplan
4. Klassenzimmer
5. Hausmeister
6. Pause
7. Buch
8. Füller
9. Schuldirektor
10. Bluse
11. Übungsheft
12. Lineal
13. Locher

my school day 2

1. Hemd
2. Krawatte
3. Biologie
4. Kantine
5. Sport
6. Französisch
7. Schulhof
8. Lehrerin
9. Geschichte
10. Chemie
11. unterrichten
12. Trimester
13. Taschenrechner

my school day 3

② **Lucy's desk**

What is on Lucy's desk? Write down the words.

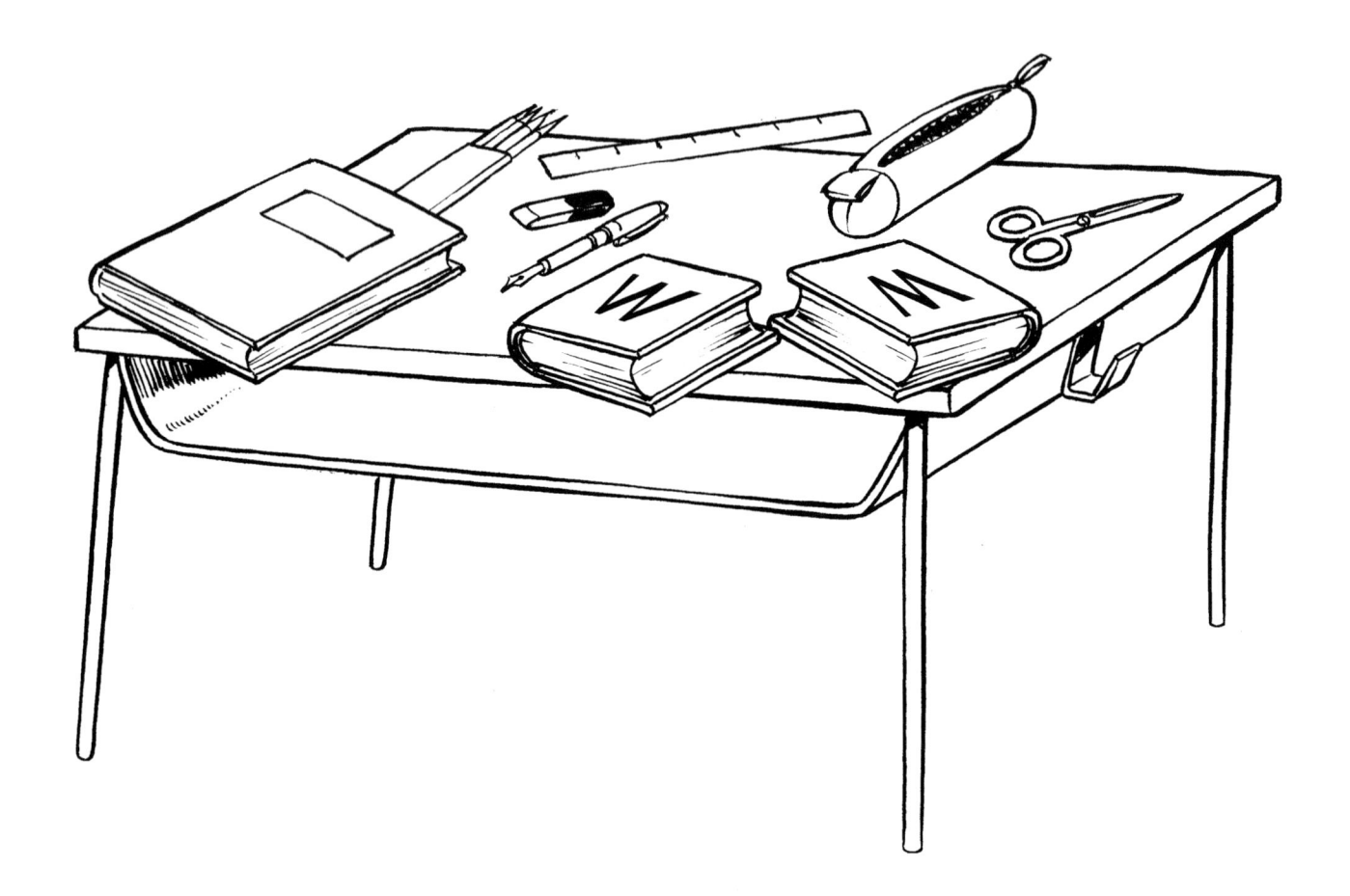

_____

_____

③ **Do you know the rooms at school? Write down the names.**

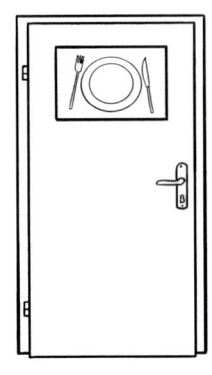

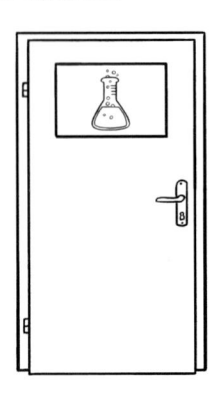

_____   _____   _____   _____

my school day 4

④ **Look at Dave's timetable and answer the questions.**

Lesson	Monday	Tuesday	Wednesday	Thursday	Friday
ASSEMBLY					
1	PE	science	geography	maths	drama
2	PE	maths	English	English	history
BREAK					
3	French	art	science	music	science
4	English	art	technology	ICT	maths
LUNCH					
5	maths	drama	ICT	history	RE

1. When is PE?

   _____

2. How many lessons does Dave have in maths?

   _____

3. When does Dave have drama?

   _____

4. Is there a geography lesson on Monday?

   _____

5. When is music lesson?

   _____

6. Does Dave learn Italian at school?

   _____

my school day 5

⑤ **My timetable**
Write your timetable.

TIMETABLE

	Monday	Tuesday	Wednesday	Thursday	Friday

my school day 6

⑥ **Write an e-mail to your English penfriend Jack and tell him about your school.**

Here are some ideas. You can write about

- your school
- your timetable
- your favourite lesson
- what you like / don't like
- your teachers
- your friends at school

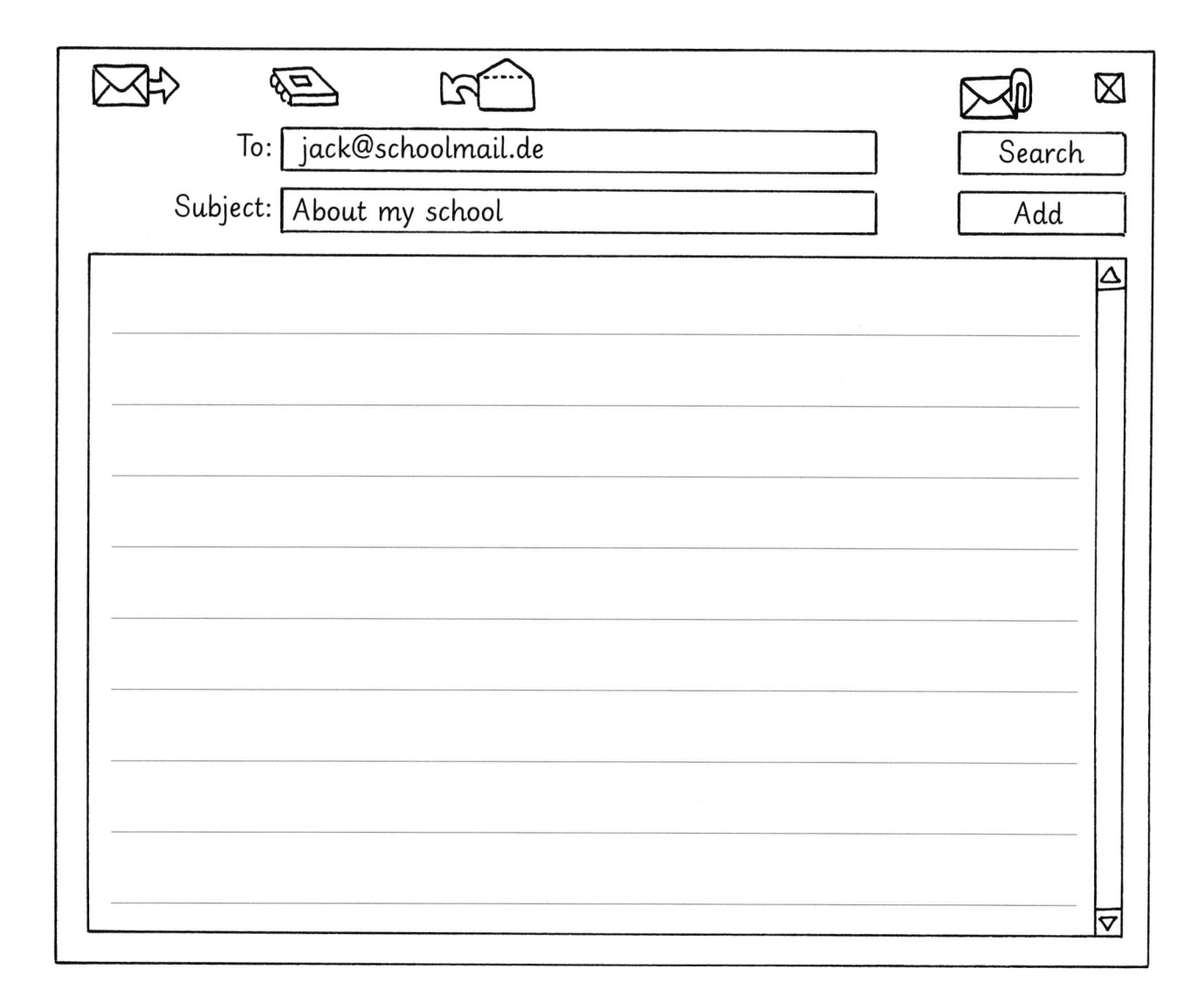

To: jack@schoolmail.de
Subject: About my school

my school day 7

⑦ **My first day at school**

Read this text and correct the sentences below.

Today was my first day at the new school. My new school is very big and my classroom has many windows. My classroom teacher is Mrs Jackson. She teaches PE and maths and I see her every day. My classmates are very nice and they show me everything. Every morning we meet at the assembly hall for registration. At this school we all wear a uniform. I don't like it very much, but I don't have to think about what I wear at school. One of the students forgot his tie today. Mrs Jackson talked to him and told him that it is one of our school rules to wear a tie. She is very strict, but nice. I love my school and my favourite subject is science. That's because of our teacher Mr Richardson. He is very funny and tells jokes all day long.

1. My new school is very small.

2. My classroom teacher is Mr Richardson.

3. At school we don't wear a uniform.

4. Every morning we meet in the sports hall.

5. My favourite subject is English.

6. Mr Richardson is strict.

3 my school day 1

❶ Crossword puzzles
Fill in the missing words.
Löse die Kreuzworträtsel.

1. Versammlung
2. Erziehung, Schulbildung
3. Stundenplan
4. Klassenzimmer
5. Hausmeister
6. Pause
7. Buch
8. Füller
9. Schuldirektor
10. Bluse
11. Übungsheft
12. Lineal
13. Locher

my school day 2

1. Hemd
2. Krawatte
3. Biologie
4. Kantine
5. Sport
6. Französisch
7. Schulhof
8. Lehrerin
9. Geschichte
10. Chemie
11. unterrichten
12. Trimester
13. Taschenrechner

my school day 3

**❷ What is on Lucy's desk?
Write down the words.
There are two more words.**

**Was befindet sich auf Lucys Tisch?
Notiere die Begriffe neben den Gegenständen.
Zwei Wörter sind zu viel.**

pen • scissors • pencil case • schoolbag • ruler • books • calculator • rubber • pencils

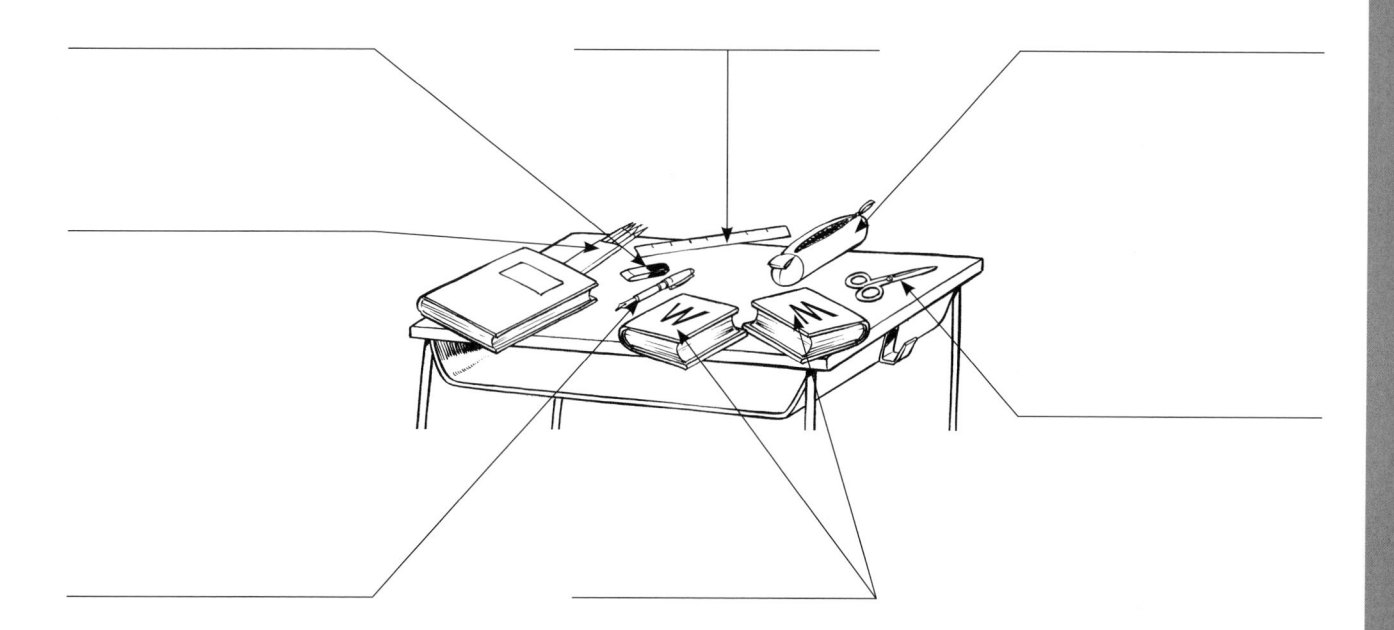

**❸ Do you know the rooms at school? Match the words with the doors.
There are two more words.**

**Kennst du die Schulräume? Verbinde die Begriffe mit den richtigen Türen.
Es sind zwei Begriffe zu viel.**

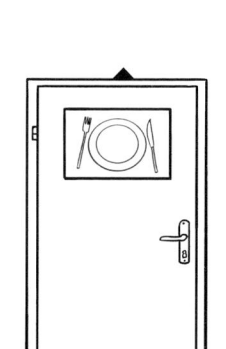

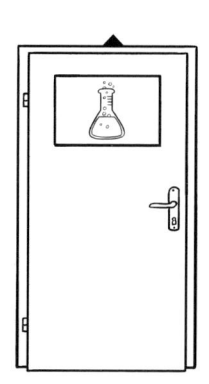

science lab • canteen • drama room • art room • computer room • sports hall

my school day 4

❹ **Look at Dave's timetable and tick the right answer.**

Sieh dir den Stundenplan von Dave an.
Kreuze die richtige Antwort an.

Lesson	Monday	Tuesday	Wednesday	Thursday	Friday
ASSEMBLY					
1	PE	science	geography	maths	drama
2	PE	maths	English	English	history
BREAK					
3	French	art	science	music	science
4	English	art	technology	ICT	maths
LUNCH					
5	maths	drama	ICT	history	RE

☐ PE is on Monday.
☐ PE is on Friday.

☐ Dave has four lessons in maths.
☐ Dave has five lessons in maths.

☐ Drama club is on Tuesday and on Wednesday.
☐ Drama club is on Tuesday and on Friday.

☐ Geography lesson is on Monday.
☐ Geography lesson is on Wednesday.

☐ Music lesson is on Tuesday.
☐ Music lesson is on Thursday.

☐ Dave learns Italian at school.
☐ Dave learns French at school.

③ my school day 5

⑤ My timetable
Write your timetable.
Use the word bank for help.

Schreibe deinen Stundenplan.
Nutze die *word bank* als Hilfe.

TIMETABLE

	Monday	Tuesday	Wednesday	Thursday	Friday

my school day 6

❻ **Write an e-mail to your English penfriend Jack and tell him about your school.**
Here are some ideas you can write about.

Schreibe eine E-Mail an deinen englischen Brieffreund Jack und erzähle ihm etwas über deine Schule.
Hier sind einige Ideen, die du verwenden kannst.

> My school is in … / great / nice.
> My timetable is … cool / not so good because …
> My favourite lesson is …
> I like … / I don't like …
> My favourite teacher is … / My classroom teacher is …
> My teachers are very nice.
> My friends at school are …

To: jack@schoolmail.de
Subject: About my school

my school day 7

① My first day at school
Read this text and correct the sentences below.

Mein erster Schultag
Lies den Text und korrigiere die Sätze unten.

Today was my first day at the new school. My new school is **very big** and my classroom has many windows. **My classroom teacher is Mrs Jackson**. She teaches PE and maths and I see her every day. My classmates are very nice and they show me everything. Every morning **we meet at the assembly hall** for registration. **At this school we all wear a uniform**. I don't like it very much, but I don't have to think about what I wear at school. One of the students forgot his tie today. Mrs Jackson talked to him and told him that it is one of our school rules to wear a tie. She is very strict, but nice. I love my school and **my favourite subject is science**. That's because of our teacher Mr Richardson. **He is very funny** and tells jokes all day long.

1. My new school is very small.

   _____

2. My classroom teacher is Mr Richardson.

   _____

3. At school we don't wear a uniform.

   _____

4. Every morning we meet in the sports hall.

   _____

5. My favourite subject is English.

   _____

6. Mr Richardson is strict.

   _____

animals and pets – word bank

wild animals	Wildtiere
tiger	Tiger
monkey	Affe
kangaroo	Känguru
crocodile	Krokodil
lion	Löwe
camel	Kamel
gorilla	Gorilla
polar bear	Eisbär
bear	Bär
bat	Fledermaus
fox	Fuchs
elephant	Elefant
snake	Schlange
hippo	Nilpferd
penguin	Pinguin
zebra	Zebra
giraffe	Giraffe

pets	Haustiere
cat	Katze
rabbit	Kaninchen
goldfish	Goldfisch
guinea pig	Meerschweinchen
bird	Vogel
dog	Hund
parrot	Papagei
puppy	Welpe

animals and pets – word bank

farm animals	Nutztiere
pig	Schwein
cow	Kuh
pony	Pony
horse	Pferd
sheep	Schaf
bull	Bulle
cattle	Rinder
chicken	Huhn
goat	Ziege
duck	Ente
goose	Gans

Where animals live / stay	Wo Tiere leben
in a cage	in einem Käfig
in an aquarium	in einem Aquarium
at the zoo	im Zoo
in a bird house	in einem Vogelhaus
on a farm	auf einem Bauernhof
at an animal shelter	im Tierheim
in a terrarium	in einem Terrarium

What animals eat	Was Tiere essen
grass	Gras
leaves	Blätter
plants	Pflanzen
insects	Insekten
fish	Fisch
meat	Fleisch
mice	Mäuse
fruits and vegetables	Obst und Gemüse

animals and pets – word bank

Animals can be …	Tiere können … sein
brown	braun
huge	riesig
small	klein
beautiful	schön
clever	schlau
wild	wild
dangerous	gefährlich
cute	niedlich

words around animals and pets	Begriffe zum Thema Tiere
(to) feed	füttern
(to) go for a walk, (to) take the dog for a walk	mit dem Hund spazieren, Gassi gehen
(to) jump	springen, hüpfen
(to) climb trees	auf Bäumen klettern
(to) catch fish	Fische fangen

animals and pets 1

① **Crossword puzzles**

1. Affe
2. Fuchs
3. Giraffe
4. Nilpferd
5. Meerschweinchen
6. Kamel
7. Tiger
8. Schlange
9. Schwein
10. Papagei
11. Käfig
12. Obst, Früchte
13. schlau
14. Rinder
15. braun

animals and pets 2

1. Katze
2. Mäuse
3. schön
4. füttern
5. niedlich
6. spazieren gehen
7. auf einem Bauernhof
8. Blätter
9. im Zoo
10. Gras
11. klein
12. Insekten
13. Bulle
14. Fledermaus
15. Eisbär

animals and pets 3

② **Write down all wild animals, pets and farm animals you remember.**

wild animals	pets	farm animals

③ **Put these animals in alphabetical order and translate.**

monkey • pony • pig • hamster • bird • cat • sheep • horse • lion • guinea pig

1. _____
2. _____
3. _____
4. _____
5. _____
6. _____
7. _____
8. _____
9. _____
10. _____

animals and pets 4

④ **Mediation**

Translate the following sentences.

1. Ein Hamster lebt in einem Käfig. _____
2. Löwen sind Wildtiere. _____
3. Kaninchen essen Karotten. _____
4. Ein Hund braucht einen Garten. _____
5. Die Katze ist schön. _____

⑤ **Write an e-mail to your friend Sophie about your pet. What does it look like and what does it do all day? If you don't have one, write about what pet you would like to have and why.**

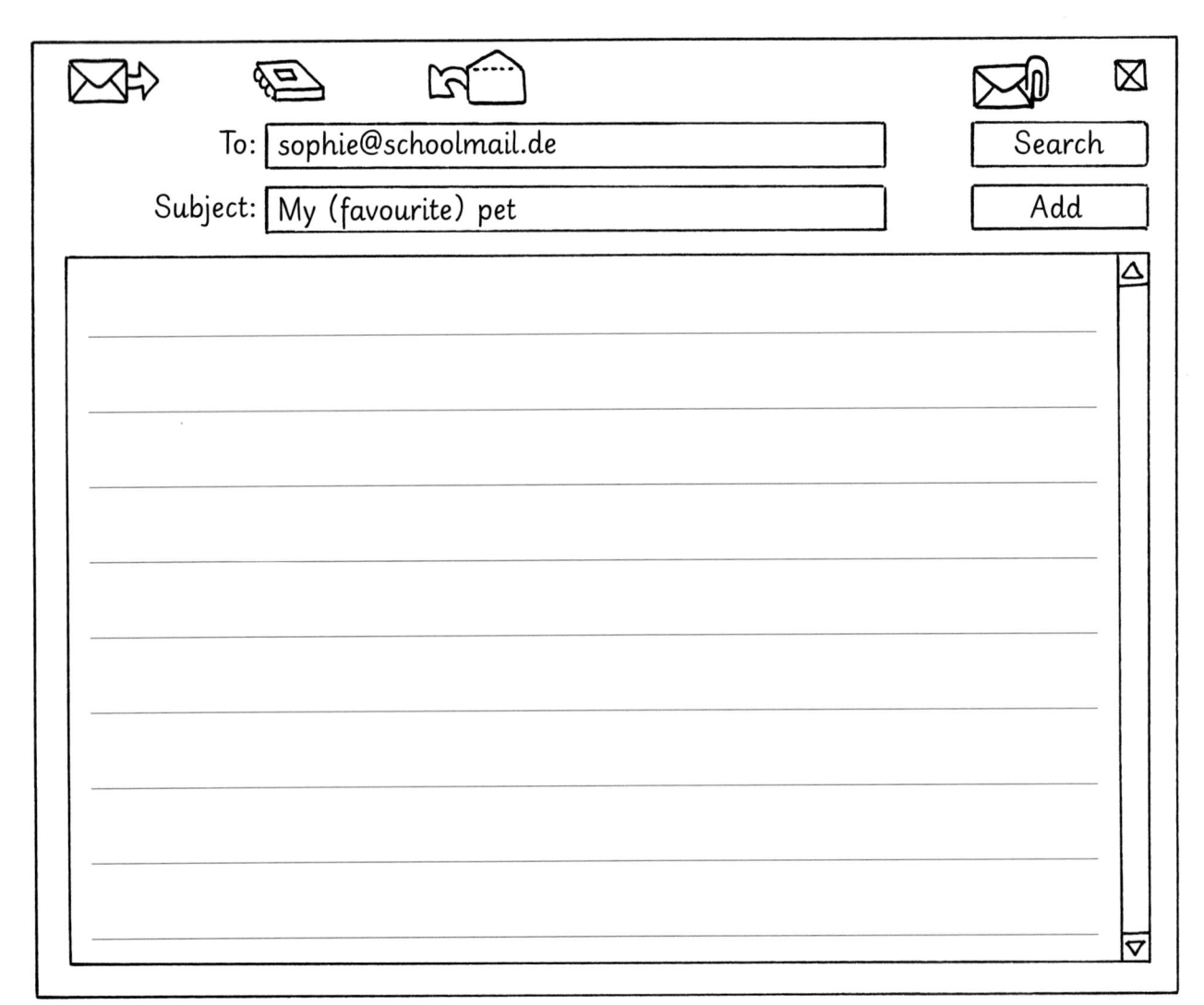

To: sophie@schoolmail.de

Subject: My (favourite) pet

animals and pets 1

❶ Find as many words about animals and pets as you can in the word puzzle and colour them.

Finde möglichst viele Begriffe zu Tieren in diesem Suchsel und markiere sie farbig.
Die fettgedruckten Anfangsbuchstaben helfen dir.

J	K	Q	G	M	X	G	V	T	G	Y	Y	O	B	U	O	K	B	G
W	O	D	Z	K	H	U	**H**	I	P	P	O	G	C	P	H	B	B	S
F	H	Z	T	P	X	**C**	A	T	T	L	E	F	N	Y	K	L	B	Q
L	K	A	B	A	R	N	G	P	D	D	N	H	T	H	J	M	**C**	Q
P	K	P	H	W	H	U	W	H	I	H	K	T	Q	F	D	**P**	A	C
T	Z	**G**	U	I	N	E	A	P	I	G	X	T	A	N	I	A	G	P
N	C	E	A	I	J	B	R	X	M	O	C	B	J	Q	L	R	E	I
X	**S**	O	G	V	F	L	S	M	L	C	F	Z	B	**F**	H	R	Q	J
B	H	R	Q	B	E	B	Q	Z	F	C	S	I	K	R	B	O	R	U
Z	E	B	B	R	G	O	I	X	E	E	**B**	J	R	U	K	T	J	T
X	L	O	F	O	Q	M	O	D	O	K	R	U	N	I	**T**	I	W	H
P	T	M	W	**G**	L	Q	S	F	Q	U	O	L	W	T	I	Q	**C**	O
Y	E	E	B	I	Z	**F**	O	X	S	B	W	D	V	P	G	W	A	H
V	R	S	I	R	C	M	R	U	G	P	N	B	N	P	E	K	M	K
H	W	W	U	A	W	**M**	O	N	K	E	Y	R	F	D	R	D	E	O
T	T	L	G	F	H	C	L	P	J	R	N	Y	F	O	X	Y	L	N
A	L	A	J	F	Y	I	R	I	**P**	T	D	**S**	N	A	K	E	S	C
K	A	N	V	E	M	V	V	H	I	D	M	O	O	M	J	B	Q	Y
B	Y	D	H	N	G	C	O	H	G	U	C	B	B	Q	F	V	D	W

animals and pets 2

❷ **Have a look at the box and write down the animal words under the right headline.**

Schau dir die Begriffe an und ordne diese der richtigen Überschrift zu.

~~elephant~~ • parrot • goldfish • ~~cattle~~ • dog • zebra • polar bear • cow • tiger • pony • hippo • puppy • chicken • snake • sheep • bull • giraffe • ~~cat~~ • duck • rabbit • guinea pig

wild animals	pets	farm animals
elephant	cat	cattle

❸ **Put these animals in alphabetical order.**

Schreibe die Tiernamen in alphabetischer Reihenfolge.

monkey • pony • pig • hamster • ~~bird~~ • cat • ~~sheep~~ • horse • lion • guinea pig

1. bird
2. _____
3. _____
4. _____
5. _____
6. _____
7. _____
8. _____
9. _____
10. sheep

animals and pets 3

④ Find the right translation.

Finde die richtige Übersetzung und verbinde.

Ein Hamster lebt in einem Käfig.	A dog needs a garden.
Löwen sind Wildtiere.	The cat is beautiful.
Kaninchen essen Karotten.	A hamster lives in a cage.
Ein Hund braucht einen Garten.	Rabbits eat carrots.
Die Katze ist schön.	Lions are wild animals.

animals and pets 4

5 **Write an e-mail to your friend Sophie about your pet.**
What does it look like and what does it do all day?
If you don't have one, write about what pet you would like to have and why.

Schreibe eine E-Mail über dein Haustier an deine Freundin Sophie.
Beschreibe sein Aussehen und was es den ganzen Tag macht.
Wenn du kein Tier hast, dann schreibe über dein Wunschtier und warum du es gerne hättest.
Nutze die Ideen aus der Box.

> I have a … / It looks … / It has … / It lives in … / It eats … /
> My favourite pet is a … / I want to have a … because …

To: sophie@schoolmail.de
Subject: My (favourite) pet

at the zoo 1

① **My favourite zoo**

Write down a short text about your favourite zoo. Explain why you like it and what is special about it. Write 60 words or more.

_____

_____

_____

_____

_____

② **A visit at the zoo**

You are in England with your family and you want to visit the zoo. There is a programme, but your parents don't understand this brochure.
Answer the questions on the following page in German.

What's on at the zoo?

- **Young visitors** (1–3)
  pay half price for their entry ticket this month.

- **For young visitors:**
  Learn about animals and feed them yourself.
  Bring your camera with you.
  You are allowed to take pictures.

- **Penguin show**
  for young and old

- **Pony riding**
  for young visitors from 3–5 o'clock.
  Please bring a helmet with you and enjoy riding
  our cute ponies. Your parents can relax
  in the café next door and have a cup of tea.

- **Animal circus show**
  A funny circus show with many
  animals and clowns.

at the zoo 2

1. Wie viel zahlen Kinder diesen Monat?

2. Gibt es ein spezielles Angebot für junge Besucher?

3. Gibt es auch etwas für Erwachsene und Kinder?

4. Was müssen wir beim Ponyreiten beachten?

5. Gibt es sonst noch eine Show?

at the zoo 1

❶ My favourite zoo

Write down a short text about your favourite zoo.
Explain why you like it and what is special about it.
Write 40 words or more.
Use the ideas in the box.

Schreibe einen Text über deinen Lieblingszoo.
Erkläre, warum du diesen Zoo besonders magst.
Schreibe mindestens 40 Wörter.
Nutze die Ideen in der Box.

> My favourite zoo is …
> I love this zoo because …
> There are … animals …
> I visit this zoo with …
> I love …
> I don't like …

at the zoo 2

② A visit at the zoo

You are in England with your family and you want to visit the zoo.
There is a programme, but your parents don't understand this brochure.
Circle the right answers and translate.

Du bist mit deiner Familie in England und ihr wollt in den Zoo gehen.
Leider verstehen deine Eltern das Programm nicht.
Kreise für sie die richtigen Antworten im Text ein und notiere diese auf Deutsch.

What's on at the zoo?

- **Young visitors** (1–3)
  pay (half price) for their entry ticket this month.

- **For young visitors:**
  Learn about animals and feed them yourself.
  Bring your camera with you.
  You are allowed to take pictures.

- **Penguin show**
  for young and old

- **Pony riding**
  for young visitors from 3–5 o'clock.
  Please bring a helmet with you and enjoy riding
  our cute ponies. Your parents can relax
  in the café next door and have a cup of tea.

- **Animal circus show**
  A funny circus show with many
  animals and clowns.

---

1. Wie viel zahlen Kinder diesen Monat? *Den halben Preis.*

2. Gibt es ein spezielles Angebot für sie? _____

3. Gibt es auch etwas für Erwachsene und Kinder? _____

4. Was müssen wir beim Ponyreiten beachten? _____

5. Gibt es sonst noch eine Show? _____

5 prepositions – word bank

PREPOSITIONS OF TIME

prepositions of time with *at*	Zeitangaben mit der Präposition *at*
at 4 o'clock	um 4 Uhr / 16 Uhr
at sunrise	bei Sonnenaufgang
at sunset	bei Sonnenuntergang
at the moment	in diesem Moment, momentan
at bedtime	zur Schlafenszeit
at midnight	um Mitternacht
at dinnertime	zur Essenszeit (abends)
at lunchtime	zur Mittagszeit (Mittagessen)
at Christmas	an Weihnachten
at once	auf einmal, gleichzeitig

prepositions of time with *in*	Zeitangaben mit der Präposition *in*
in May	im Mai
in summer, in winter	im Sommer, im Winter
in 2022	in 2022
in the next century	im nächsten Jahrhundert
in the past, in the future	in der Vergangenheit, in der Zukunft
in the morning	am Morgen, morgens
in the middle ages	im Mittelalter

prepositions of time with *on*	Zeitangaben mit der Präposition *on*
on Monday	am Montag
on Mondays	montags
on 7th May	am 7. Mai
on Christmas Day	am 1. Weihnachtstag
on Independence Day	am Tag der Unabhängigkeit
on my birthday	an meinem Geburtstag
on New Year's Eve	an Silvester
on Easter Monday	am Ostermontag

5 prepositions – word bank

> Bei Zeit- und Ortsangaben ändert sich die Präposition. Beachte bei folgenden Ausdrücken die Schreibweise!

in	on
in the morning	*ABER* **on** Tuesday morning
in the mornings	**on** Saturday mornings
in the afternoon(s)	**on** Sunday afternoon(s)
in the evening(s)	**on** Monday evening(s)

at	to
(to) be **at** work	(to) go **to** work
(to) be **at** a party, to be **at** a match	(to) go **to** a party, to go **to** a match
(to) be **at** home	⚠ (to) go home

Hier sind noch weitere Ausdrücke mit feststehender Präposition:

in a newspaper	in der Zeitung
in the middle of …	mitten in, in der Mitte von …
in a car, taxi, bus	im Auto, Taxi, Bus
in the sky	am Himmel
at home	zu Hause
at work	auf der Arbeit
at a party, at a concert	auf einer Party, auf einem Konzert
at a hotel	in einem Hotel
on the first floor	im ersten Stock

5 prepositions – word bank

PREPOSITIONS OF PLACE

in front of the box	**behind** the box	**in, inside** the box	**outside** the box
on the chair	**on top of** the closet	**on** the wall	**at** the table
			by, near the chair
(a)round the camp fire	**over** the table	**under** the desk	**above, below** their sibling
between the dogs	**opposite** the dog	**with** the dog	**among** the dogs
at the the greengrocer's	**at** school	**in** bed	**in** the street

© PERSEN Verlag

75

prepositions – word bank

PREPOSITIONS OF DIRECTION

(to) turn left	links abbiegen
(to) turn right	rechts abbiegen
(to) go straight on	geradeaus gehen / fahren
at the end of the street	am Ende der Straße
How do I get to …?	Wie komme ich zu …?
Excuse me, can you tell me the way to …?	Entschuldigen Sie, können Sie mir den Weg nach / zu … erklären?

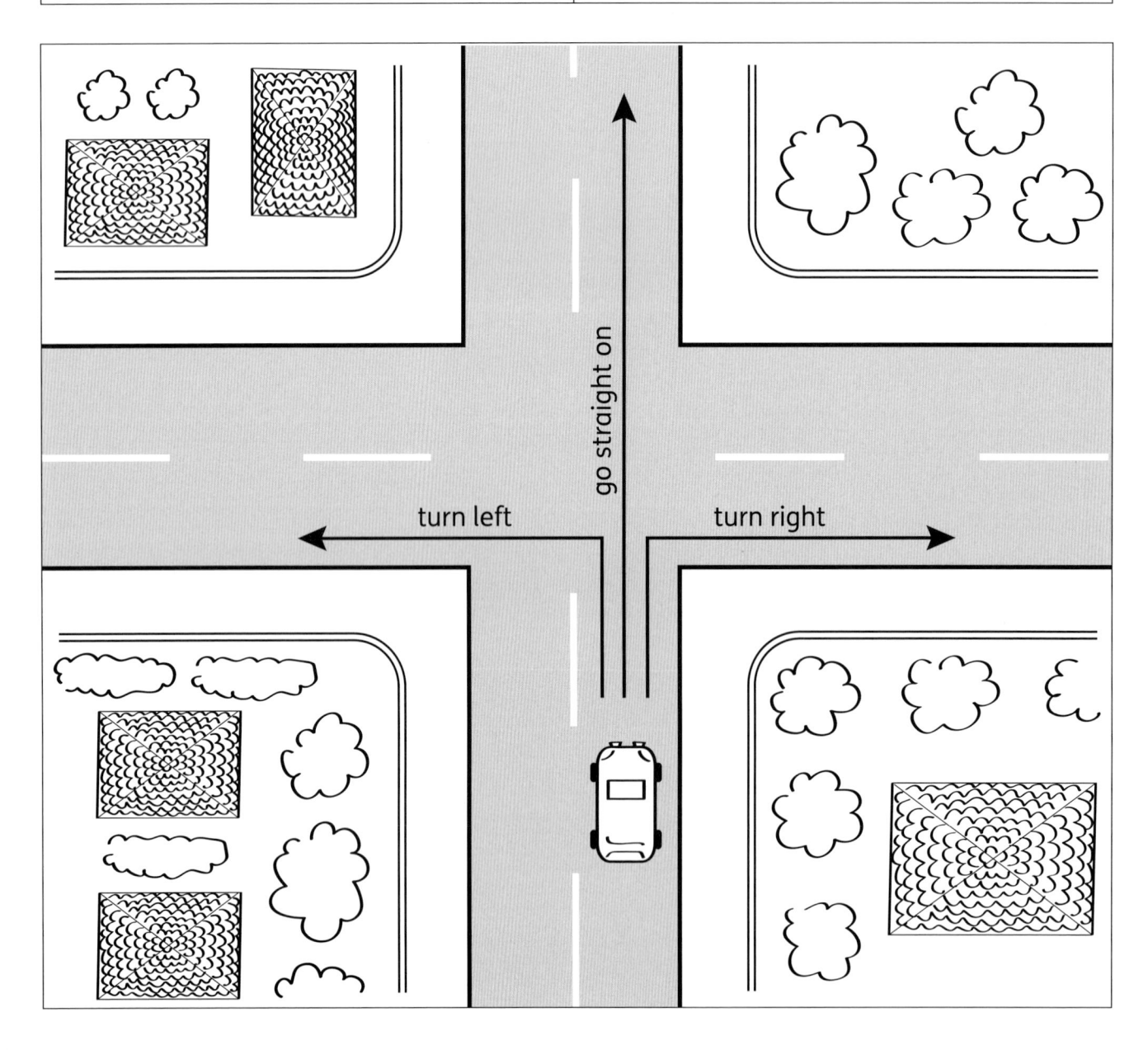

prepositions – word bank

VERBS WITH PREPOSITIONS

verbs + preposition	Verben + Präposition
(to) ask for sth	nach etwas fragen, um etwas bitten
(to) belong to	zu … gehören
(to) happen to	passieren
(to) listen to (the radio, teacher)	(dem Radio, der Lehrkraft) zuhören
(to) talk to sb about sth (to) speak to sb about sth	mit jdm. über etwas sprechen
(to) thank sb for sth	jdm. für etwas danken
(to) wait for	auf … warten
(to) think about sth	über etwas nachdenken
(to) think of sth or sb	an etwas oder jdn. denken
(to) look at sth	etwas anschauen
(to) look for sth	nach etwas suchen
(to) look after sb	sich um jdn. kümmern

prepositions 1

① **Fill in the missing prepositions: *at / in / on*.**

1. I have a conference _____ 8 am.

2. School starts _____ half past 8.

3. In Brazil it often rains _____ summer.

4. He went to the park _____ lunchtime.

5. He works _____ Mondays.

6. The family watches a movie _____ the weekend.

7. There will be a lot to do _____ the coming weeks.

8. I am sure we will visit Mars _____ the future.

9. _____ my birthday I will have a pool party.

10. Mother's day is _____ May.

11. Her birthday is _____ 26th April.

12. I will be with my friends _____ New Year's Day.

13. The shops open _____ Mondays.

14. There is no school _____ Sundays.

15. I will have a good job _____ the future.

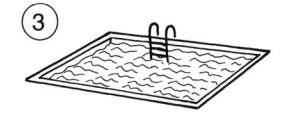

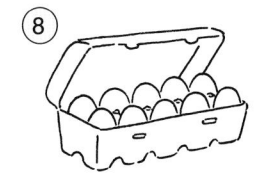

prepositions 2

② Look at the pictures and answer the questions.

1. Where is the man? <u>The man is in the kitchen.</u>
2. Where is the bus? _____
3. Where can you swim? _____
4. Where is the water? _____
5. Where is the person standing? _____
6. Where are the posters hanging? _____
7. Where are the flowers? _____
8. Where are the eggs? _____
9. Where are the horses? _____
10. Where are the sweets? _____

prepositions 3

③ **Look at the pictures and answer the questions briefly. Have a look at the example.**

1. Where are they? <u>At the party.</u>
2. Where is he sleeping? _____
3. Where is she? _____
4. Where is the boy? _____
5. Where is the man? _____
6. Where are the girls? _____
7. Where is the man? _____
8. Where can we find stars? _____
9. Where is the parrot? _____
10. Where is the car? _____

prepositions 4

④ Fill in at / on / in.

1. Did you have a lot of fun _____ the party last night?
2. My parents are _____ their friend's house.
3. My grandmother is _____ hospital.
4. Who is your cousin _____ this picture?
5. Did you work _____ this project?
6. Are you _____ home now?
7. I am sure there will be many people _____ the concert next week.
8. Who is the best football player _____ this world?
9. I met nice people _____ my way here.
10. We are going to meet _____ the cinema.
11. My sister lives _____ Denmark.
12. The number is _____ that paper.
13. There is a cat _____ the roof.
14. There is a poster _____ the wall.
15. There are many pages _____ this book.
16. Please don't sit _____ the table.

⑤ Fill in to or in.

1. I love eating _____ my bed.
2. My family is flying _____ Munich next month.
3. I need to go _____ school.
4. Does this bus go _____ the centre?
5. I want to live _____ London.
6. I go _____ bed very late.
7. I stay _____ my bed too long.

prepositions 5

⑥ **Where are the people in the picture?**
Complete the sentences with: *behind / next to / in front of.*

1. Becky is sitting _____ Adam.

2. Adam is sitting _____ Lucy.

3. Tom is sitting _____ Marc.

4. Daniela is sitting _____ Tom.

5. Adam is sitting _____ Becky.

prepositions 6

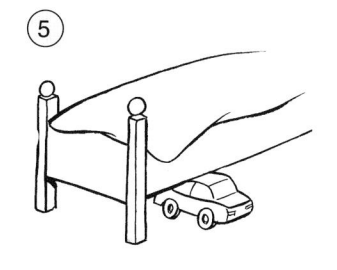

Look at the pictures and complete the sentences with the right preposition.

1. The dog is _____ the table.

2. The boy is standing _____ the wardrobe.

3. The chair is standing _____ the computer.

4. His free hand is _____ side.

5. The car is _____ the bed.

6. The boy is sitting _____ the computer.

7. The boy is standing _____ the door.

8. The girl is sitting _____ the boy.

prepositions 7

⑧ **Look at the pictures and complete the sentences with the right preposition (*to / for / at*). Choose an end for the sentences. Think of the word bank „VERBS + PREPOSITION".**

1. The boys are listening _____.

2. The people are waiting _____.

3. The students are looking _____.

4. The man is looking _____.

5. The girl is talking _____.

6. The woman is looking _____.

84

prepositions 1

1 Fill in the missing prepositions: *at*, *in*, *on*.
Entscheide dich für die richtige Präposition und kreise ein.

1. I have a conference **in / at** 8 am.
2. School starts **in / at** half past 8.
3. In Brazil it often rains **on / in** summer.
4. He went to the park **at / on** lunchtime.
5. He works **on / at** Mondays.
6. The family watches a movie **at / on** the weekend.
7. There will be a lot to do **in / at** the coming weeks.
8. I am sure we will visit Mars **at / in** the future.
9. **At / On** my birthday I will have a pool party.
10. Mother's day is **in / on** May.
11. Her birthday is **in / on** 26th April.
12. I will be with my friends **at / on** New Year's Day.
13. The shops open **at / on** Mondays.
14. There is no school **in / on** Sundays.
15. I will have a good job **in / on** the future.

prepositions 2

❷ Look at the pictures and answer the questions.
Schau dir die Bilder an und beantworte die Fragen.

1. Where is the man? <u>In the kitchen.</u>

2. Where is the bus? _____

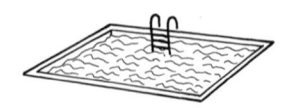

3. Where can you swim? _____

4. Where is the water? _____

5. Where is the person standing? _____

6. Where are the posters hanging? _____

7. Where are the flowers? _____

8. Where are the eggs? _____

In the box.

~~In the kitchen.~~

In the swimming pool.

On the floor.

On the table.

At the window.

On the wall.

At the bus stop.

prepositions 3

3 Look at the pictures and answer the questions.
Schau dir die Bilder an und beantworte die Fragen.

1. Where are they?

    At the party.

    | In the sky. |

2. Where is he sleeping?

    _____

    | ~~At the party.~~ |

3. Where is she?

    _____

    | In his bed. |

4. Where is the man?

    _____

    | On the road. |

5. Where is he?

    _____

    | In the bathroom. |

6. Where can we find stars?

    _____

    | In the cage. |

7. Where is the parrot?

    _____

    | At her desk. / At work. |

8. Where is the car?

    _____

    | In the train. |

prepositions 4

4 Which preposition is right: *at / on / in*?
Entscheide dich für die richtige Präposition und kreise sie ein.

1. Did you have a lot of fun **at / on** the party last night?
2. My parents are **in / at** their friend's house.
3. My grandmother is **at / in** hospital.
4. Who is your cousin **on / in** this picture?
5. Did you work **at / in** this project?
6. Are you **in / at** home now?
7. I am sure there will be many people **at / in** the concert next week.
8. Who is the best football player **on / in** this world?
9. I met nice people **on / in** my way here.
10. We are going to meet **on / at** the cinema.
11. My sister lives **at / in** Denmark.
12. The number is **on / in** that paper.
13. There is a cat **at / on** the roof.
14. There is a poster **at / on** the wall.
15. There are many pages **at / in** this book.
16. Please don't sit **on / at** the table.

5 Which preposition is right: *to* or *in*?
Entscheide dich für die richtige Präposition und kreise sie ein.

1. I love eating **to / in** my bed.
2. My family is flying **to / in** Munich next month.
3. I need to go **to / in** school.
4. Does this bus go **to / in** the centre?
5. I want to live **to / in** London.
6. I go **to / in** bed very late.
7. I stay **to / in** my bed too long.

prepositions 5

**❻ Which sentences are right?
Tick the correct sentences.**

**Welche Sätze sind richtig?
Kreuze an.**

☐ Becky is sitting behind Adam.
☐ Adam is sitting behind Daniela.

☐ Adam is sitting next to Tom.
☐ Adam is sitting next to Lucy.

☐ Marc is sitting in front of Adam.
☐ Tom is sitting in front of Marc.

☐ Daniela is sitting next to Tom.
☐ Daniela is sitting next to Lucy.

☐ Adam is sitting in front of Becky.
☐ Becky is sitting in front of Tom.

prepositions 6

**❼ Look at the sentences and find the right picture.
Write the number of the sentence next to the picture.
Circle the preposition in the sentence.**

**Lies die Sätze und finde die dazugehörigen Bilder.
Schreibe die richtige Nummer neben das Bild.
Kreise im Satz die Präposition ein.**

1. The chair is next to the computer.
2. The girl is sitting opposite the boy.
3. The boy is sitting in front of the computer.
4. His free hand is on the right side.
5. The boy is standing next to the door.
6. The dog is under the table.
7. The car is under the bed.
8. The boy is standing behind the wardrobe.

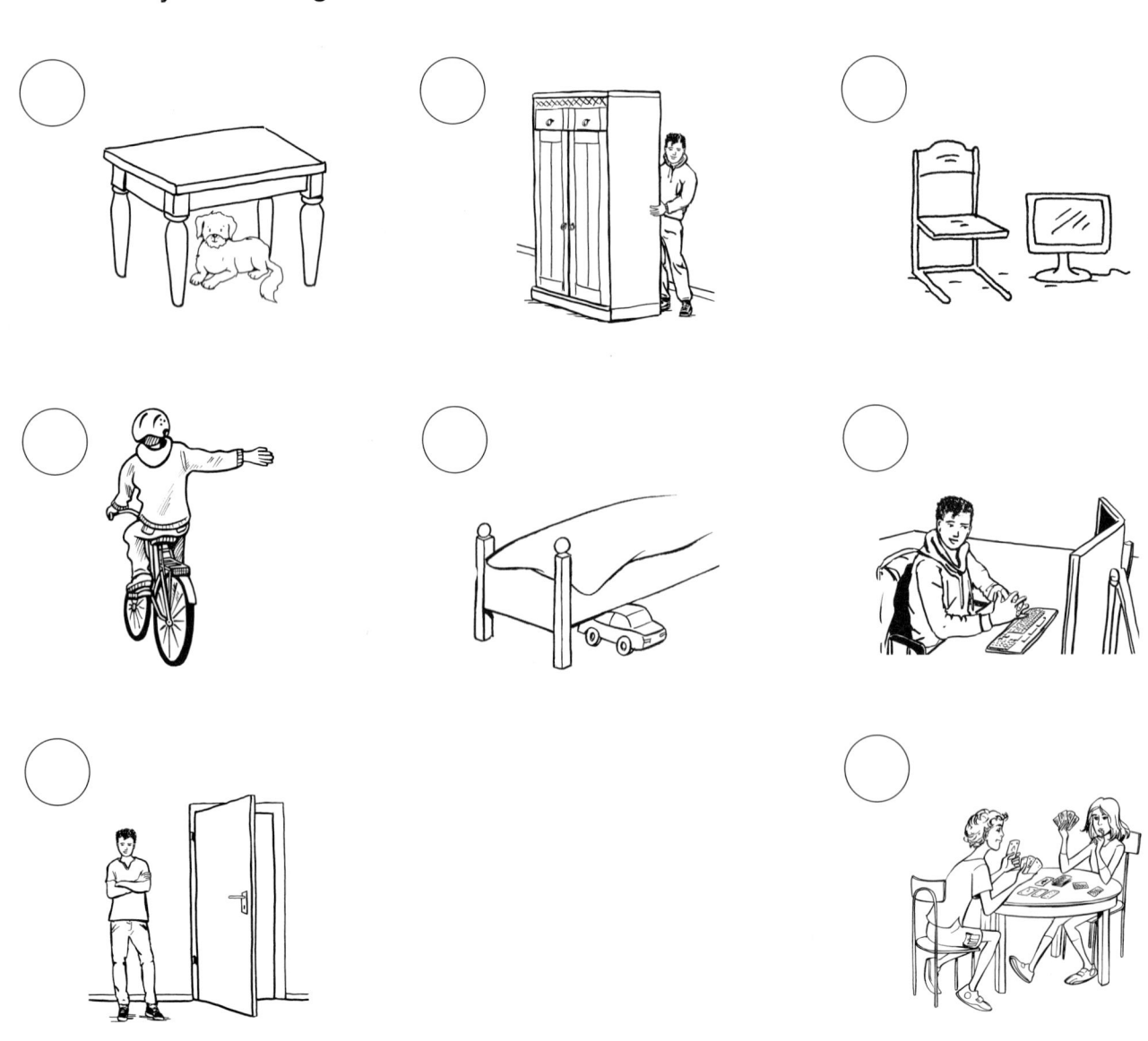

prepositions 7

8 Look at the picture and complete the sentences with the right preposition. Take the word bank „VERBS + PREPOSITION" for help and circle the right preposition.

Schau dir die Bilder an und vervollständige die Sätze mit der richtigen Präposition.
Nimm die *word bank* „VERBS + PREPOSITION" zu Hilfe und kreise die richtige Präposition ein.

1. The boys are listening **to** / **at** the radio.

2. The people are waiting **for** / **to** the doctor.

3. The students are looking **at** / **to** an experiment.

4. The man is looking **to** / **at** the dog.

5. The girl is talking **to** / **for** her friend.

6. The woman is looking **to** / **at** the clock.

numbers – word bank

1 one	2 two	3 three	4 four	5 five	6 six	7 seven	8 eight	9 nine	10 ten
11 eleven	12 twelve	13 thirteen	14 fourteen	15 fifteen	16 sixteen	17 seventeen	18 eighteen	19 nineteen	20 twenty
21 twenty-one	22 twenty-two	23 twenty-three	24 twenty-four	25 twenty-five	26 twenty-six	27 twenty-seven	28 twenty-eight	29 twenty-nine	30 thirty
31 thirty-one	32 thirty-two	33 thirty-three	34 thirty-four	35 thirty-five	36 thirty-six	37 thirty-seven	38 thirty-eight	39 thirty-nine	40 forty
41 forty-one	42 forty-two	43 forty-three	44 forty-four	45 forty-five	46 forty-six	47 forty-seven	48 forty-eight	49 forty-nine	50 fifty
51 fifty-one	52 fifty-two	53 fifty-three	54 fifty-four	55 fifty-five	56 fifty-six	57 fifty-seven	58 fifty-eight	59 fifty-nine	60 sixty
61 sixty-one	62 sixty-two	63 sixty-three	64 sixty-four	65 sixty-five	66 sixty-six	67 sixty-seven	68 sixty-eight	69 sixty-nine	70 seventy
71 seventy-one	72 seventy-two	73 seventy-three	74 seventy-four	75 seventy-five	76 seventy-six	77 seventy-seven	78 seventy-eight	79 seventy-nine	80 eighty
81 eighty-one	82 eighty-two	83 eighty-three	84 eighty-four	85 eighty-five	86 eighty-six	87 eighty-seven	88 eighty-eight	89 eighty-nine	90 ninety
91 ninety-one	92 ninety-two	93 ninety-three	94 ninety-four	95 ninety-five	96 ninety-six	97 ninety-seven	98 ninety-eight	99 ninety-nine	100 one hundred

numbers – word bank

Achte auf die Schreibweise:

4 = four	14 = fourteen	40 = forty
5 = five	15 = fifteen	50 = fifty

Hunderterzahlen

100 = a hundred / one hundred

200 = two hundred

300 = three hundred

400 = four hundred

500 = five hundred

600 = six hundred

700 = seven hundred

800 = eight hundred

900 = nine hundred

1000 = a thousand / one thousand

Merke:

- Vor *hundred* steht immer „a" oder ein Zahlwort!
- Zwischen *hundred* und anderen Zahlwörtern steht immer „and"

Beispiel:

110 = one hundred **and** ten

220 = two hundred **and** twenty

numbers 1

① **Quiz**

Each line is missing some numbers. Fill in the missing numbers.

1 one	2 two	___	4 four	5 five	6 six	7 seven	___	9 nine	10 ten
___	12 twelve	___	14 fourteen	15 fifteen	___	17 seventeen	18 eighteen	___	20 twenty
twenty-one	22 twenty-two	23 twenty-three	___	25 twenty-five	26 twenty-six	27 twenty-seven	28 twenty-eight	29 twenty-nine	___
31 thirty-one	32 thirty-two	___	34 thirty-four	___	36 thirty-six	37 thirty-seven	38 thirty-eight	39 thirty-nine	40 forty
___	42 forty-two	43 forty-three	___	45 forty-five	46 forty-six	___	48 forty-eight	49 forty-nine	___
52 fifty-two	52 fifty-two	53 fifty-three	54 fifty-four	___	56 fifty-six	57 fifty-seven	58 fifty-eight	59 fifty-nine	50 fifty
61 sixty-one	62 sixty-two	___	64 sixty-four	65 sixty-five	___	67 sixty-seven	68 sixty-eight	69 sixty-nine	___
71 seventy-one	72 seventy-two	73 seventy-three	74 seventy-four	75 seventy-five	___	77 seventy-seven	78 seventy-eight	79 seventy-nine	70 seventy
81 eighty-one	___	83 eighty-three	84 eighty-four	85 eighty-five	86 eighty-six	___	88 eighty-eight	89 eighty-nine	90 ninety
91 ninety-one	92 ninety-two	___	94 ninety-four	95 ninety-five	96 ninety-six	___	98 ninety-eight	___	___

numbers 2

② **Write down the numbers.**

18 _____

44 _____

64 _____

112 _____

88 _____

346 _____

13 _____

36 _____

25 _____

741 _____

③ **Choose 5 numbers and tell your partner. He/She should write them down. In turn he/she should choose 5 numbers that you write down. Look at the first example.**

my numbers	my partner's numbers
116	(152) one hundred and fifty-two

numbers 1

❶ Quiz

Each line is missing some numbers.

Notiere die fehlenden Zahlen in jeder Zeile.
Verwende zur Hilfe die *word bank*.

	2 two		4 four	5 five	6 six	7 seven		9 nine	10 ten
one									
	12 twelve		14 fourteen	15 fifteen		17 seventeen	18 eighteen		20 twenty
21 twenty-one	22 twenty-two	23 twenty-three		25 twenty-five	26 twenty-six	27 twenty-seven	28 twenty-eight	29 twenty-nine	
31 thirty-one	32 thirty-two		34 thirty-four		36 thirty-six	37 thirty-seven	38 thirty-eight	39 thirty-nine	40 forty
	42 forty-two	43 forty-three		45 forty-five	46 forty-six		48 forty-eight	49 forty-nine	50 fifty
	52 fifty-two	53 fifty-three	54 fifty-four		56 fifty-six	57 fifty-seven	58 fifty-eight	59 fifty-nine	
61 sixty-one	62 sixty-two		64 sixty-four	65 sixty-five		67 sixty-seven	68 sixty-eight	69 sixty-nine	70 seventy
71 seventy-one	72 seventy-two	73 seventy-three	74 seventy-four	75 seventy-five		77 seventy-seven	78 seventy-eight	79 seventy-nine	
81 eighty-one		83 eighty-three		85 eighty-five	86 eighty-six		88 eighty-eight	89 eighty-nine	90 ninety
91 ninety-one	92 ninety-two		94 ninety-four	95 ninety-five	96 ninety-six		98 ninety-eight		

numbers 2

2 Write down the numbers.
Notiere die Zahlen.

eighteen _____

forty-four _____

sixty–four _____

one hundred and twelve _____

eighty-eight _____

three hundred and forty-six _____

thirteen _____

thirty-six _____

twenty-five _____

seven hundred and forty-one _____

3 Choose 5 numbers and tell your partner.
He/She should write them down.
In turn he/she should choose 5 numbers that you write down.
You can use the word bank for help. Look at the first example.

**Suche dir 5 Zahlen aus und notiere sie.
Dein Partner oder deine Partnerin soll die Zahlen mithilfe der *word bank*
aufschreiben und dir ebenfalls 5 Zahlen nennen.
Schreibe diese Zahlen mithilfe der Tabelle auf. Achte auf das Beispiel.**

my numbers	my partner's numbers
116	*(152) one hundred and fifty-two*

the date – word bank

Geschriebenes Datum	Gesprochenes Datum
January 1st 1st January	January the first the first of January
February 22nd 22nd February	February the twenty-second the twenty-second of February
March 23rd 23rd March	March the twenty-third the twenty-third of March

DIE ORDNUNGSZAHLEN

1. = 1st / the first	11. = 11th / the eleventh
2. = 2nd / the second	12. = 12th / the twelfth
3. = 3rd / the third	13. = 13th / the thirteenth
4. = 4th / the fourth	14. = 14th / the fourteenth
5. = 5th / the fifth	15. = 15th / the fifteenth
6. = 6th / the sixth	16. = 16th / the sixteenth
7. = 7th / the seventh	17. = 17th / the seventeenth
8. = 8th / the eighth	18. = 18th / the eighteenth
9. = 9th / the ninth	19. = 19th / the nineteenth
10. = 10th / the tenth	20. = 20th / the twentieth

the date – word bank

The months	Die Monate
January	Januar
February	Februar
March	März
April	April
May	Mai
June	Juni
July	Juli
August	August
September	September
October	Oktober
November	November
December	Dezember

Beachte:
- ✔ Das Datum wird anders gesprochen, als es geschrieben wird.
- ✔ Die Ordnungszahl kann vor oder hinter dem Monat stehen.
- ✔ Vor der Jahreszahl steht ein Komma.
  Beispiel: April 15th, 2022.
- ✔ Die Monatsnamen werden immer großgeschrieben.

the date 1

① **Write the English date.**

15.04.2021 _____

01.03.2019 _____

23.04.1998 _____

27.07.1995 _____

19.12.2020 _____

02.05.1989 _____

② **Write the German date.**

March 1st, 2020 _____

September 22nd, 1999 _____

August 14th, 2021 _____

May 23rd, 1999 _____

November 4th, 1975 _____

December 16th, 1992 _____

April

Monday 25

Tuesday ♡ 26
Yvonne's birthday

Wednesday 27

Thursday 28

the date 2

③ **Create your family & friends birthday calendar and note the English date.**

mum	**dad**
date: _____	date: _____

sister / brother
date: _____

sister / brother
date: _____

family

grandmother
date: _____

grandfather
date: _____

aunt
date: _____

uncle
date: _____

cousin
date: _____

name: _____
date: _____

name: _____
date: _____

friends

name: _____
date: _____

name: _____
date: _____

name: _____
date: _____

name: _____
date: _____

name: _____
date: _____

the date 1

**❶ Find the right dates.
There are two more than you need.**

**Finde die richtigen Daten und verbinde sie.
Zwei sind zu viel.**

① 15.04.2021

② 01.03.2019

③ 23.04.1998

④ 27.07.1995

⑤ 19.12.2020

⑥ 02.05.1989

Ⓐ 23rd August, 1998
August 23rd, 1998

Ⓑ 15th April, 2021
April 15th, 2021

Ⓒ 2nd May, 1989
May 2nd, 1989

Ⓓ 19th December, 2020
December 19th, 2020

Ⓔ 27th July, 1995
July 27th, 1995

Ⓕ 2nd May, 2019
May 2nd, 2019

Ⓖ 1st March, 2019
March 1st, 2019

Ⓗ 23rd April, 1998
April 23rd, 1998

1	2	3	4	5	6

Übrig: _____

❷ Find the right date and write it down.

Finde das richtige Datum in der Box und notiere es.

04.11.1975 • 14.08.2021 • 23.05.1999 • 01.03.2020 • 16.12.1992 • 22.09.1999

March 1st, 2020 _____   May 23rd, 1999 _____

September 22nd, 1999 _____   November 4th, 1975 _____

August 14th, 2021 _____   December 16th, 1992 _____

the date 2

❸ **Create your family & friends birthday calendar and note the English date. Use the word bank for help.**

Erstelle einen Family-&-Friends-Kalender und notiere jeweils das englische Datum.
Verwende hierfür die *word bank*.

mum
date: _____

dad
date: _____

sister / brother
date: _____

sister / brother
date: _____

grandmother
date: _____

grandfather
date: _____

family

cousin
date: _____

name: _____
date: _____

name: _____
date: _____

friends

name: _____
date: _____

name: _____
date: _____

name: _____
date: _____

name: _____
date: _____

name: _____
date: _____

English in action – word bank

How to (dis-)agree with somebody	Jdm. zustimmen / widersprechen
That's a great idea.	Das ist eine großartige Idee.
That's right.	Das ist richtig.
Good idea!	Gute Idee!
I agree (with you).	Ich stimme (dir) zu.
I don't agree (with you).	Ich stimme (dir) nicht zu.
That sounds great.	Das klingt großartig.
You are right.	Du hast recht.
I like …, too.	Ich mag … auch.
Well, I don't think so.	Ich finde nicht.
That's (not) true.	Das ist (nicht) wahr.

How to ask for sth	Um etwas bitten
Can I (call my parents), please?	Kann ich bitte (meine Eltern anrufen)?
Can I have …, please?	Kann ich bitte … haben?
May I …, please?	Könnte / Dürfte ich bitte …?
I'd like …, please.	Ich hätte gerne …, bitte.
Can you …, please?	Kannst du bitte …?

How to suggest sth	Etwas vorschlagen
Let's …	Lass uns …
Come on, let's …	Los, lass uns …
What about …?	Wie wäre es mit …?
Why don't you …?	Wieso … nicht …?
What do you think?	Wie denkst du darüber?
Don't you think?	Denkst du nicht?

CLASSROOM PHRASES

What the teacher says	Anweisungen der Lehrkraft
Please open your books at page …	Öffnet bitte eure Bücher auf Seite …
Turn to page … please.	Blättert bitte zu Seite …
Look at line …	Seht euch die Zeile … an.
Look at the next paragraph.	Schaut euch den nächsten Absatz an.
Read the text.	Lest den Text.
Listen to …	Hört euch … an.
Listen to track number …	Hört euch Nummer … an.
Work on page …	Arbeitet auf Seite …

English in action – word bank

What the teacher says	Anweisungen der Lehrkraft
Work in pairs.	Arbeitet zu zweit.
Work in groups of four.	Arbeitet zu viert.
Sit in a circle.	Bildet einen Sitzkreis.
Write about …	Schreibt über …
Talk about …	Sprecht über …
Ask questions.	Stellt Fragen.
Answer the questions.	Beantwortet die Fragen.
Write down the answers.	Notiert die Antworten.
Match the sentences.	Ordnet die Sätze zu.
Come to the board, please.	Kommt bitte an die Tafel.
Collect … please.	Sammelt bitte … ein.
Do this exercise at home, please.	Erledigt diese Aufgaben bitte zu Hause.
Be quiet, please.	Seid bitte ruhig.
Sit down, please.	Setzt euch bitte.
Please hurry up.	Bitte beeilt euch.
Please speak up.	Sprecht bitte lauter.
Try again.	Versucht es noch einmal.
That's right / wrong.	Das ist richtig / faslch.
Well done.	Gut gemacht.
You can do better.	Das könnt ihr besser.

English in action – word bank

If there is a problem	Wenn es ein Problem gibt
Sorry, I'm late.	Entschuldigung, ich bin zu spät.
Sorry, I've forgotten my book.	Entschuldigung, ich habe mein Buch vergessen.
Sorry, I haven't done my homework.	Entschuldigung, ich habe meine Hausaufgaben nicht gemacht.
What's the matter?	Was ist los?
Can / May I open the window, please?	Kann / Dürfte ich bitte das Fenster öffnen?
I feel sick.	Ich fühle mich krank.
Can / May I go to the toilet, please?	Kann / Dürfte ich bitte zur Toilette gehen?
I've got a problem with …	Ich habe ein Problem mit …

If you need help	Wenn ihr Hilfe braucht
Can you help me, please?	Können Sie / Kannst du mir bitte helfen?
I've got a question.	Ich habe eine Frage.
I don't understand …	Ich verstehe nicht …
How can I do this exercise?	Wie mache ich diese Aufgabe?
What's … in English / German?	Was heißt … auf Englisch / Deutsch?
What does … mean?	Was bedeutet …?
Can you write it on the board, please?	Können Sie / Kannst du das bitte an die Tafel schreiben?
Can you say that again, please?	Können Sie / Kannst du das bitte wiederholen?
Can you spell that, please?	Können Sie / Kannst du das bitte buchstabieren?
Sorry, I don't know.	Entschuldigung, ich weiß es nicht.
What page, please?	Welche Seite bitte?

English in action – word bank

If you work together	Wenn ihr miteinander arbeitet
Whose turn is it?	Wer ist dran?
It's my turn.	Ich bin an der Reihe.
Do you want to work with me?	Möchtest du mit mir arbeiten?
Can I work with you?	Kann ich mit dir arbeiten?
Let's check …	Lass uns … überprüfen.
Let's compare …	Lass uns … vergleichen.
Let's act out the dialogue.	Lass uns den Dialog vorspielen.
Let's change roles.	Lass uns die Rollen tauschen.

If you work with the computer	Wenn ihr am Computer arbeitet
Do you have an e-mail address?	Hast du eine E-Mail-Adresse?
Click on this link.	Klicke auf diesen Link.
Follow this link.	Folge dem Link.
Can I download / upload it?	Kann ich es herunterladen / hochladen?
I saved it.	Ich habe es gespeichert.
My computer has crashed.	Mein Computer ist abgestürzt.

classroom phrases 1

① **Things you might say to your teacher**

Write down the phrases. Think of two more phrases that you need in classroom and fill in the table.

Du möchtest wissen, ob etwas richtig ist.	
Die Lehrerin soll etwas wiederholen.	
Du brauchst Hilfe.	
Du fragst nach der Bedeutung eines Wortes.	
Du verstehst etwas nicht.	
Du hast deine Hausaufgaben nicht gemacht.	
Du hast dein Buch vergessen.	
Du fragst nach der Seite im Buch.	
Du fragst, wie du die Aufgabe lösen kannst.	
Du bittest den Lehrer, das Wort zu buchstabieren.	
Du möchtest zur Toilette.	

classroom phrases 2

② **Things your teacher might say to you**

Write down the phrases. Think of three more phrases that your teacher can say in English and fill in the table. Give the table to your partner. He / She should translate it into German.

Lies bitte den Text.	
Schlage dein Buch auf.	
Arbeitet zu zweit.	
Komm bitte zur Tafel.	
Wo sind deine Hausaufgaben?	
Erledige diese Aufgabe bitte zu Hause.	
Das ist richtig.	
Schreibe die Antworten auf.	
Wer möchte den Text vorlesen?	
Sammelt bitte die Bücher ein.	

classroom phrases 1

❶ Things you might say to your teacher

Cut out the pieces and find the right pairs.

Dinge, die du zu deinem Lehrer sagen könntest

Schneide die Felder aus und finde die richtige Übersetzung.

Du möchtest wissen, ob etwas richtig ist.	Can you repeat it, please?
Der Lehrer soll etwas wiederholen.	Is that right?
Du brauchst Hilfe.	Sorry, but I've forgotten my book.
Du fragst nach der Bedeutung eines Wortes.	I'm sorry, I don't understand.
Du verstehst etwas nicht.	Can / May I go to the toilet, please?
Du hast keine Hausaufgaben.	What does that mean in English?
Du hast dein Buch vergessen.	Can you spell it, please?
Du fragst nach der Seite im Buch.	I don't have the homework.
Du fragst, wie du die Aufgabe lösen kannst.	What page, please?
Du bittest den Lehrer, das Wort zu buchstabieren.	How can I do this exercise?
Du möchtest zur Toilette.	I need help.

classroom phrases 2

❷ Things your teacher might say to you

Find the right translations and connect the sentences.

Dinge, die deine Lehrerin sagen könnte

Finde die richtige Übersetzung und verbinde die Sätze miteinander.

Lies bitte den Text.	Where is your homework?
Schlage dein Buch auf.	Write down the answers.
Arbeitet zu zweit.	That's right.
Komm bitte zur Tafel.	Work in pairs.
Wo sind deine Hausaufgaben?	Please come to the board.
Erledige diese Aufgabe bitte zu Hause.	Read the text, please.
Das ist richtig.	Do this exercise at home, please.
Schreibe die Antworten auf.	Collect the books, please.
Wer möchte den Text vorlesen?	Please open your book.
Sammelt bitte die Bücher ein.	Write about …
Schreibe über …	Who wants to read the text?

8 classroom phrases 3

Tandem time

Cut out the two pieces of this and the next page and play the tandem game.

Schneidet die zwei Karten auf diesem und dem nächsten Blatt aus und spielt das Spiel im Tandem.

classroom phrases 1	classroom phrases 2
Suche dir eine Partnerin oder einen Partner. Wer den deutschen Satz hat, muss diesen übersetzen. Der Partner/die Partnerin kontrolliert die Übersetzung. Wenn ihr bei dem letzten Satz angekommen seid, tauscht die Seiten des Bogens und fangt von vorne an.	Suche dir eine Partnerin oder einen Partner. Wer den deutschen Satz hat, muss diesen übersetzen. Der Partner/die Partnerin kontrolliert die Übersetzung. Wenn ihr bei dem letzten Satz angekommen seid, tauscht die Seiten des Bogens und fangt von vorne an.
Tut mir leid, dass ich zu spät bin.	Sorry, I'm late.
I'm fine.	Mir geht's gut.
Ich fühle mich krank.	I feel sick.
What's for homework?	Was haben wir als Hausaufgabe auf?
Kann ich bitte das Fenster öffnen?	Can I open the window, please?
Wer ist dran?	Whose turn is it?
Ich habe mein Buch vergessen.	I've forgotten my book.
Can I go to the toilet, please?	Kann ich bitte zur Toilette gehen?
Was ist los?	What's the matter?

classroom phrases 3

Du bist dran!	It's your turn!
Tut mir leid, ich habe meine Hausaufgaben nicht dabei.	Sorry, I haven't got my homework with me.
Lies bitte den Text vor.	Please read the text.
Bildet einen Sitzkreis.	Sit in a circle.
Open your books at page 34.	Öffnet eure Bücher auf Seite 34.
Arbeitet zu zweit.	Work in pairs.
Answer the question, please.	Beantwortet bitte die Frage.
Wer möchte den Text vorlesen?	Who wants to read the text?
Write down the answers.	Schreibt die Antworten auf.
Blättert zu Seite 10.	Turn to page 10.
Read the text on page 55.	Lies den Text auf Seite 55.
Seht euch Zeile 4 an.	Look at line 4.

Alle Unterrichtsmaterialien
der Verlage Auer, PERSEN und scolix

» **jederzeit online verfügbar**

lehrerbuero.de
Jetzt kostenlos testen!

Und das Beste: Schon ab zwei Kollegen können Sie von der günstigen **Schulmitgliedschaft** profitieren!

Infos unter: **lehrerbuero.de**

» lehrerbüro

Das **Online-Portal** für Unterricht und Schulalltag!